TRANSFORMATIONS

Nearing the End of Life:
Dreams and Visions

by

Phyllis Stowell

CHIRON PUBLICATIONS • ASHEVILLE, NORTH CAROLINA

Author photo by Deborah O'Grady © 2019

www.ChironPublications.com

Interior and cover design by Danijela Mijailovic
Printed primarily in the United States of America.

ISBN 978-1-63051-724-3 paperback
ISBN 978-1-63051-725-0 hardcover
ISBN 978-1-63051-726-7 electronic
ISBN 978-1-63051-727-4 limited edition paperback

Library of Congress Cataloging-in-Publication Data Pending

*The spectacle of old age would be unendurable did we not
know that our psyche reaches into a region held captive
neither by change in time nor by limitation of place.
In that form of being our birth is a death and our death a birth.*

C. G. Jung

*Dreaming is the flickering activity of the mind
participating in the world's imagination.*

James Hillman

PREFACE

In the beginning, the listener was a mature woman wearing silver earrings. In time, her voice blurred with others, including my own. I came to her after a dream of an attic fire. I thought of the reprobate who hid in the church basement, wondering if it was he whose fury burned down fields and farmhouses in my dreams.

I assumed our meetings would extend a week or two until my anxiety eased. I would drive calmly day or night, and all would be well, not as last midnight, when I turned left toward an unlit street. Out of hell a bicyclist darted into my headlights. I was the one least skilled on the Everest climb who slipped, dragging four others downward, arms and legs splayed to grasp the cliff face, to cling where nothing was.

ALSO by PHYLLIS STOWELL

BOOKS

Ascent to Solitude
Arc of Grief
Engraved Tablet
SHIELD/Bouclier
Engraved Tablet
SUNDERED
A Cast of Coins

CHAPBOOKS

Who is Alice?
Emergence

ANTHOLOGY
Co-editor
APPETITE:
Food as Metaphor
An anthology of Women Poets

CONTENTS

GNOSIS

ORGAN SYMPHONY

AS I HAVE DONE

IMMERSE YOURSELF

Like the two opposing wings of a butterfly, the dream-world is one wing and the awake world is the other wing. The butterfly must have both wings connected at the Heart in order to fly.

Dreams are direct, incorruptible expression of the mysterious nature of life and are considered [by the Mayan's] to be free of human connivance.

Dreams call upon life to move and live.

Martin Prechtel

Blue Pearls

After my husband Jerry's death, I felt that I did not know how to give my life what it lacked. Like Pousette-Dart, who had to leave the New York art scene before his paintings could become his own, I knew I must move away, away from the way I inhabited the world. I worried about a life lasting too long, about falling short of what I should be or become. I told the listener I did not know how to release myself from being driven, how to free myself from harmful obsessions, long-gone battles and defeats.

You must get through this before you die.

Then came a prescient dream:

> A lovely woman holds out for me a dress studded with blue pearls.

The Serpent

And after I had seen this apparition, I woke and I said to myself:
What is the cause of this vision?

Zosimos

In a bright courtyard I wait, then an older man wearing blue Persian pants and shirt leads me into a dark, rich-hued interior. He sits down, signals me to sit opposite him. In silence he studies me, his face deeply grooved and desert-weathered, his eyes penetrating. At our feet a circular pool of sand. Abruptly, he leaps up and thrusts his cane into its center. It begins to bend and sway. To my horror it rises up before me, an enormous serpent with glittering scales. Its unblinking eyes stare as it weaves over our heads. Then it begins to unfurl wings.

This vision came when I was alone in the dark, sitting in a deep meditative state. I did not know what the serpent was but knew I was meant to know. I felt its primordial power that filled me with paralyzing awe.

This serpent is chthonic, of the underground from which it rises and to which it returns. It strikes instinctively regardless of the effect, on others, on you.

This is in me? I shuddered.

Scraps of This and That

At an intersection a man wearing black glasses driving a red Ferrari pulled up to the right of my car, his ultra-motor revving. Knowing he would cut in front of me where the lanes merged, I waited for the light to yellow, charged, and, heart thumping, forced him to fall behind—my car barely missing a pedestrian crossing ahead midblock.

That night I dreamed a circular lead rod slowly rotated in the sky while twelve smaller replicas circled around it.

Lead is a base metal, a sign of depression, a leaden mood. The rod is in the heavens, and the constellation is in motion.

> A poet holding his rejected and revised poems, one on currant-red parchment, hands me a translucent sheet with four perfectly proportioned primary colors.

> A man takes over a woman's studio, projecting his images onto hers.

> Dining among poets without a knife, I eat scraps of this and that.

These dreams came in three successive nights. In grief, I told my friend, who with dismay answered, *You don't realize how much you have accomplished*—she herself a woman who, blocked in her career, altered her life and grew into rare red oak visited by ravens.

A Box of Pins

A man hands me a cup, and thirsty I walk toward the fountain, but as I walk toward it, it sinks. I walk lower, again it sinks. Each time I near it, it sinks further until I stop in despair.

A child is born without eyes.

A child cannot see what is wrong. A child accepts, adapts.

As a child, I lingered long hours among the dust motes in the tower attic of the parsonage, a spacious, drafty Victorian. I loved it. Like James Hillman, who was allowed an attic room of his own, this was my private place. I was free to imagine *anything*.

All was not well. Hillman was not neglected.

A tiger lies next to me on a velvet sofa, his body warm and comforting, his pelt pattern uniquely his own.

My friend lets me give her pet Bengal tiger water from a black hose. He lets me massage behind his ears. I think of William Blake's *Tyger*. This could be primordial dark burning, could be imagination, could be both.

The male tiger is not related. He's a loner.

I was very little, standing, looking up at my father when my cherished bronze-green elephant dropped between us and shattered.

I was inundated with dreams. In one, a woman is a perfectionist. Marion Woodman, a minister's daughter like me, said in an interview that being Preacher's Kid put pressure on her to be perfect. When I was kicked out of Sunday School, I was told rebellion was typical of P K's.

I spill a box of sewing pins, gold ones mixing with silver ones. There are so many I am disheartened.

I must sort the dreams, offer only the gold ones.

Molting

One day I removed my wedding band, moving my engagement ring to my middle finger, thinking perhaps I will find a new love. Then I thought, No, this is about finding myself, who I was from the beginning.

A young man gleefully spray-paints walls and doorframes red and black. He is arrested. I enter a barn where a tied-up bull means to have sex. I edge past him. Two men grab me, forcing my arms behind my back. Released from prison, the young man rescues me.

I am sitting beside a man driving a Chris Craft, the water parting and swirling after us. Ahead in a blinding orange light I discern a cluster of boats with people leisurely lounging. He speeds around them, then the water narrows. It darkens. We approach whitish green fog. I am afraid.

In these dreams both the blinding orange-drenched light and the greenish-white fog suggest an alchemical process is being activated.

~

A woman next to me falls or is pushed. She plummets to her death on the stone landing below.

I was alarmed, afraid I had done something terrible.

This death is good.

She smiled, offered no explanation.

I was among strangers in a complex of rooms. My black and white purse with my car keys and identity card was stolen. I looked everywhere, frightened, then climbed two flights of increasingly narrow stairs where people with masks wore weird costumes, a Fellini's *Satyricon*. I swiveled around, rushed back down.

To come down is essential.

I enter an elevator and push the button for the seventh floor, where Jerry is. It goes berserk, zipping up and down. Frantically I push different buttons. When it stops, I get out in a basement at the back entrance where men are shoveling garbage from a large funnel into a truck bin.

Well that's down, I thought.

Coming to the High Sierras

I kill a small green Pegasus, as if it were an insect.

Kill a tiny winged horse! A Pegasus? beautiful Pegasus who emerged from mother Medusa's neck when she was beheaded. His hoof cracked open Mt. Helicon and the spring burst forth—spring of the muses, source of inspiration. Never!

You killed it because it was inadequate.

Parallel bars in a vertical plane, two rows of three each, each containing a message—most ordinary but one labeled *Imagining My Future* intrigues me. I hesitate. *Read it*, urges a quiet man beside me.

In my journal: *I must find where my poems belong, find where I fit.*

I carry my manuscripts through the rain walking to James Hillman's house. His wife is wearing black, as I am. I come a second time. We both wear crimson. Smiling, this time she takes the manuscripts. I say *These belong to James.*

James Hillman's writings reflect his insight that image-making itself is the key—to aesthetics, to the psyche, to life.

~

As I leave the dark wooded interior of a restaurant-bar in the high Sierras, the owner with a sagacious look hands me a bouquet of stark white narcissus and one hundred one-hundred- dollar bills. I am pleased but bewildered.

He is giving you what you have lacked from childhood, both pure self-love and the value of wholeness.

That's hard to believe. I remember childhood! How I loved running through the rotating yard sprinkler naked, loved the barn swing, loved dressing up for Easter, parading myself (unseen) before mother's bedroom mirror in an orange, ruffled organdy dress. I had two playmates.

Sometimes we do not remember the problems of childhood. It is one way the psyche protects the self. Even if you do not remember, that past can influence your life in a harmful way. This dream is significant. It offers much more than happiness.

Before You Die

Jung's *Red Book* is displayed in a house where people roam. Then alone in an attic dusty with old furniture, I hear a deep, masculine voice from *The Red Book* speaking to me. A stranger in black enters looking for me. He sits on the sofa, and I leave. When I return, he has fallen asleep. Now I am wearing black, but on the back is a blood red cross.

There is a parallel life, a dream theater. Like Jung's *Red Book*, is this the beginning of my own slightly mad trip?

Standing opposite a man in a black suit, I remove my cloak with a cross on the back and drape it over my arm. He hands me a goblet of dark liquid, telling me to drink it. It tastes like a mixture of zinfandel and blood. I follow a gowned figure down a monastic hallway. He leaves me in a cell with a small high window, a cot, a chair and a lit candle on a square stand. I lay the garment onto the cot and sit a long time contemplating the red cross, then stare in terror as it begins to move, morphing into a fiery snake.

What, if attacked by this snake, I suffer real agonies but nothing in me or in my life transforms?

~

My son and I had a dispute.

Be in your Buddha self when you are with him. I hear bitterness in your voice.

After conflict with my daughter, I dreamt of a cockroach in a rose.

The cockroach has no feeling; when you do not feel your own anger, it kills the rose. You act strong so even those close to you aren't aware of the hurt you suffer.

The next day my back went into spasm. I rolled on the floor, called no one. In my mind the 16th-century friar Giordano Bruno burning at the stake in Rome, his mouth sealed.

You must get through this. I have seen horrors. At the time of death, screaming.

Unpacking

In a French-speaking country having left a B & B hungry,
I am driving the wrong way on a one-way road. When I
get to the village where I am supposed to stay at a poetry
residency, in halting French I ask directions from a well-
dressed woman in her fifties who disdainfully turns
away. I enter a library filled with teenagers lounging
about and smooching couples on sofas. An odd-looking
fellow, apparently the librarian, wearing a pair of huge
magnifying glasses, lies on the floor helping some students.
Leaving, I bump into a young man and hold out my open
palm saying, *Excuse me*. He changes from being annoyed
to being pleased. It is getting late, and I become anxious,
then discover I have lost my purse and foolishly had not
worn my travel belt, so everything was gone—passport,
money, license.

Unpacking the dream:

French is a language I have never mastered, so I am in the territory
of my inadequacy. A haughty Frenchwoman's disdain for me now
lives inside my mind. The B & B, where one is supposed to rest
and be fed, fails me and, leaving, I am hungry. Whatever works
for everyone, no longer satisfies me. Driving, I am going against
agreed-upon conventions or simply going the wrong way.

The great Library of Humanity has been degraded as a hangout
for kids, and the Librarian, archetypally a spiritual guide to the
wisdom of ages, is on his knees, wearing magnifying glasses and
can only see what is smack in front of his face.

When I respond to the man with openness, he becomes
responsive. Late and anxious, I have lost my identity in a foreign
country. Day doesn't wipe away the nightwood of dream.

The Feminine

My friend had claimed credit for work I had done. I told her. She didn't see it that way. We discussed it, then let the subject drop.

That's feminine relatedness. She has a good, extroverted perception, and you benefit by staying related to her. Like siblings, you give your spirit and energy together and are accomplishing valuable work in the world.

My daughter and I have packed to leave. The house is empty except a few things in the closet. I take my best blanket, leaving the rest for her. We are going separate ways.

Psychological separation can be difficult, but it is better for both mother and daughter to part ways.

A disabled older man is being taken care of by a younger woman. I cannot be responsible for him and leave the house. Outside I decide I cannot take the long route by which I have come.

The feminine is not the mother, not the nurse for an old man. The feminine is love of life and the carrier of life-giving water.

Immerse Yourself

In a house with others I call an analyst who in the past had seen my husband. Old, hunched over, he comes to the phone. I tell him I am worried about Jerry's depression. I sense he is dying and cannot talk for himself. The analyst mumbles something, then shouts *Destroy all the wine!* which upsets me because we have a lot of bottles for a party I am about to host. I can hear them being broken.

Jerry was not depressed, even the last months of his dying. Old age and death dead ahead, and I'm planning a party?

Jerry tells me he has found letters I wrote to Hitler. He shows me one. It's his letter. I peak through the bedroom curtains, nervous that others might see us naked. It is dark. No one is outside.

Jerry would say we are all mad and Hitler is in all of us. I don't understand this dream.

This much is clear, you are not done with grief.

In a foreign country I am carrying a bag of groceries I want to return. I walk up and down a steep cobbled street, searching for the store—T N Task. An old woman wearing a multi-colored shawl tells me to go farther down inside the complex.

The dream distressed me—my persistent mismatch with time, my endless mistakes, the pervasive sense that I do not know my way, that I'm caught in a sea change beyond control. How frightening that something I do not know in me is explosive, something used for war or demolition. Who has the power to defuse it? *My* task?

~

Suspended in space, a glistening black shark. I stare at it, standing beside a man whose first wife had been a victim of abuse. Suddenly it dives, disappearing into dark water.

The fish stared at me with an eerie cold eye—death? Something dreadful of which I am unaware? Something ominous, chilling...

~

A baby's muffled cry. I find her in an upper bunk above her mother, who is deep in sleep. She's tightly bound in a blanket, something like Saran wrap wound over her head and face. When I unwrap and bathe her, a milky gray substance sticks to her skin. I give her a bottle, the nipple cut to release quick fluid. She gulps, desperately.

You identify with that infant. What is helpful to acknowledge is your caring response.

I discover that a couple who bought the house that had been Jerry's and mine had plastered over its ancient stone fireplace, replacing it with an artificial one. Outside, near their garden, I lie down in a bathtub filling with clear spring water. When the water reaches my chin, the husband pushes down on my head. I struggle with him, then he forces me down.

I woke, alarmed.

Their fireplace isn't the warm soulful hearth you and Jerry shared. Since his death, you have been attacked by these two interior characters who are murderous, cruel, unfeeling, and unrelated.

A chained, black Labrador with a metal collar tries to come to me. At a potluck dominated by an egotistical woman, I felt isolated and ignored. When it grows dark,

I look for my sterling silver forks, but they are gone. A young man in mourning is playing the piano.

Awake on and off all night, up too early.

Immerse yourself in this. Let the images unfold.

FATAL DISEASE

Deeply ingrained in the infantile psyche is the conscious or unconscious assumption that the cure for depression is to replace it with pleasant, happy feelings, whereas the only valid cure for any kind of depression lies in the acceptance of real suffering.

Helen Luke

It is only when the innocent core of the dis-integrated self is allowed to suffer that the imprisoning enclave of Hell is broken open.

Donald Kalsched

Neptune's Daughter

A gray dove probes where the pain is. She dislodges a black and white stone.

The dove, spirit of love, descending to be embodied ... but always white. Gray—a blend of opposites. Black stone white stone—yin and yang? good and evil? Why does this stone cause pain?

My neighbor with flowing fiery red hair, mother of Orion, shows me a rose-gold wedding ring.

My former neighbor's sons are named after constellations. Rose-gold, like my mother's wedding rings. Perhaps there was in my redheaded mother a quality that saved me despite what she could not give? How ambiguous all this is!

In gray dawn an ornate gilded coach approaches, traveling at a slow, dignified pace. When it nears, I see a bearded Neptunelike figure standing, holding a scepter. A seven-year-old girl steps out of the coach, invites me to ride with her. I get in, sit beside her, then find myself in her palatial bedroom. *You need clean clothes*, she says, scowling. Amazed, I see how dirty and ragged I am. She shows me her books and drawings, tells me the king (whom I saw standing in the coach) is her father, but she rarely sees him. One day she will be as important as he is.

The night after this vision, I dream my friend who paints by the sea holds out in her graceful hand a necklace of shells.

This necklace replicates your first dream of the blue pearl dress, but you can't integrate her gift because you are caught. This father is the god of the sea, only instead of the trident, he carries a scepter as symbol of his power, a power your father held in his young daughter's eyes. This identification can create inflation and a drive for impossible achievement.

Yearning

What you yearn for is what you are.

James Hillman

Crossing the street in the dark, two blinding headlights
speed toward me.

I am seventy-seven. Dead ahead—death.
I make a list:
>   bone aches   arthritis
>   trigger thumb
>   ring finger bending like a claw
>   ear static scratchy, high-pitched decibels ringing

I yearn for silence

>   I can't unscrew a jar
>   can't unpeal a medicine bottle seal
>   can't spring up from the floor
>   can't balance on one foot
>   can't bike over a stone bridge passing a field of red poppies

I yearn for strength

>   I can't run, can't jump, can't remember
>   can't can't can't

Out loud, as old folks do, I say to myself, *Let go of it all!* Old
conflicts, old losses, old fine times. Too much good brings nothing
but nostalgia, dissatisfaction, longings.

>   Parked in my driveway a silver Jaguar.

A magical dream. Yes, I yearn to be Miranda, Prospero's daughter!
Not Neptune's, not Saturn's.

Soulfulness

Many pianists in parallel rows are performing a Beethoven sonata. During the pause between the second and third movements, I pass lit candles for listeners to hold as they stand beside the pianists' benches.

Beethoven transformed suffering into art that moves us. The dream felt holy, religious.

My daughter and I are writing at a small Paris cafe table. Watching a white bird in water that reflects a tissue-yellow sky, I try to describe the effect of it. A poet arrives who, when her brother died, became an owl. I want her to join us, but we can't because a gray-scarfed man has taken over our table. We go outside. Again, I see the white bird.

Compelled

As arranged, I wait impatiently at the entry, but my friend does not leave her kitchen where she is cooking for herself, only for herself.

She is a good shadow, she is attending to her own needs. She exists in you, but you are not aware of her. What compels you to attend to others instead of yourself?

My father's constant care was for others. He rose for breakfast and left after the news to make house calls for the everyone who needed attention, and church work (which included adding a block-sized addition to the church for a children's chapel, a program / auditorium, a practice room for the choirs, a Junior church, and numerous Sunday school rooms). He stopped home for a quick lunch and a brief nap, returning for an hour for dinner followed by more house calls, returning in time for the ten o'clock news. Saturday, he prepared his sermon at the church in his extensive library, which included works by Thomas Mann and Karl Menninger. Sunday, he orchestrated two services and greeted over two hundred, most of whom he knew well. After Sunday dinner with the family, he carried flowers to parishioners in the hospital. Sunday evenings were given to "University of Life" for young adults or some other event. Despite all this activity, most of his energy went to caring for others. He was widely beloved for his compassionate attention. It was who he was, it was his life.

Stick of Fire

There is no place that does not see you.

Rilke

Everywhere the alchemical fire, everywhere the eye of God.

Edinger

A field of small marks vibrating organize themselves into
two circles, two owl eyes.

The owl sees me. The tallest spruce with Spanish moss dripping
from its dying branches sees me. The white clay tinged with
shades of ochre sees me—my shovel blade, my footprint. But not
God. At Oberlin, my first year away from home, the God I had
ardently prayed to on my knees beside my bed became an
illusion, a betrayal.

*It goes back farther. Something that happened to you as a child made
the church impossible.*

A familiar man whose features I cannot discern precisely
is teaching me how to fit stained glass into a lead frame.

Fit together as in a sanctuary rose window or Chartres' stained
glass casting their hues into the interior.

Outside, after hearing a poet read what the rulers had
done to him, his suffering told with humility and gentle
humor, a woman turns her head to her left, and her
amazed face glows. I turn, look too late to flee that
violent, numinous light.

35

Magdalen, that moment in garden when the resurrected god calls to her. The next night came this dream:

> A woman leads me to lie down naked under an open skylight. Moonlight pours warmly over me, then she takes me outside, and I see a cross of brilliant stars. Suddenly, something thumps hard on my back. Turning, I face a monstrous, fiery, igneous-black, almost human shape with immense wings. His features demonic, his mouth malformed, his eyes malevolent. He exudes hate and fierce energy. She draws a curtain closed, concealing him.

I could not expunge him, as if he is—always. A cosmic demon who tears apart the departing soul? An evil divinity?

> A man says, *Here is the traffic pattern* – in the center a circle from which radiate lines circled by larger and larger circles, extending. . . .

This is a symbol of the Self—whole, still and in motion, one and multiple. Impersonal. Such images often come when we are threatened with chaos.

> I have been driving with my right-hand glove on my left hand. The glove is twisted.

You twist your creative life, trying to make it function in the world, to solve your yearning.

> My spine is a stick of fire.

Black and White

A man embraces me. I remove my black coat.
A woman who had dismissed me and my poems carries
them carefully in a white box.

Once I watched Sufis whirl. As each Sufi approached, the Master
removed the black cloak, symbol of mortality, symbol of human
limitation. Then one by one, each began to turn, joining the
turning circle of whirling white skirts, one hand raised to receive,
the other hand lowered to release into the world the spirit they
have gathered.

Azul and the Derelict

A man calls. He is coming, wait. His name—Azul.

Azul recalls Amahl—his crutch, which, being poor, is all he can give to the divine child. The miracle—his being healed. Like the miracle of the Juggler of Notre Dame, who offered her his juggling, and she smiled.

Azul in Spanish means blue, which in typology is the color of thinking. Thinking has been your crutch, but when you get agitated, unreliable thinking gets you in trouble.

Blue sky, blue spirit, blue mood, Mood Indigo.

A poet, a dry alcoholic, who is expert at self-promotion, embraces me but distains my three-pearl ring. The nacre has begun to peel. Looking for my poetry, I go down through a trapdoor. A derelict huddled in the basement corner on a pile of dirt and trash leaps up pointing a red gun. Shoots, causing an explosion and fire.

I worry about wine.

You don't have a problem with wine. That poet who gave up wine and forces his way toward recognition does not like the pearls, the feminine in you. You are right to reject him.

In the basement I ask the derelict who he is. *Your father's brother.* He has exposed his penis, but I ignore it and ask why his gun is red. He tells me he has been in our house a long time and knew me when I was a child. He has a bottle of cheap Red Eye wine. I persuade him to come upstairs into our spacious, old-fashioned kitchen. I give him a sandwich and a small glass of wine. He tells me he's from the Depression. I suggest a bath, which he takes but he won't put on my father's clothes. We go into my brother's room, where I open drawers looking for a sweater. He

38

grabs a large brass key from the bottom drawer, then takes me to a chest in the attic, which he unlocks. It's empty. I had imagined it would be filled with memorabilia. *No*, he says emphatically *It's empty!* As he leaves, he says *the gun is a toy.*

My father's father died when he was four. When he was a teenager, his oldest brother drove him off the family's Nebraska sugar beet farm. Our Victorian kitchen was in La Cross, where I was born at the peak of the Depression. The chest in the attic held family pictures. How does this fit together?

Hold the emptiness. Don't rush around trying to fill it.

Dipped in Acid

Just as I begin to read a new poem, a woman takes over with energetic effusion—her work, her affairs, her politics, her world.

Often this woman dismisses me as if I weren't there.

She's your shadow. Here she is compensatory for what you lack.

You have to dip it in acid three times.

In alchemy acid is used to dissolve what's solidified. The repeated process separates the elements.

Dressed in robes, worshippers arrive in a cathedral. When they begin a Catholic ceremony, I leave. Outside in pitch dark I ask someone where I can go. Before she can answer, a grotesque creature attaches itself to her. This happens three times. I will have to find my own way.

Borders

A huge pile of shit in the basement, my Herculean task.

A little girl—me—crawling into bed with my grown-up self.

A factory for an ointment that will make leather glossy with an unusual perfume. Sold in a black bottle with a white label that says LABEL. A man shows how it is made. The ingredient boiled human.

Hold the little girl's hand all the time. She is with you. You cannot change the past, cannot change what happened to her.

Mother promises but leaves. When she returns, upset, I say *I thought we were going to lunch. We still are,* she answers, then admits she ate with the others. And paid the bill. Angrily I exclaim, *All of them could buy and sell you three times over.*

Mother ...my mother gave my sister, who was four years older than I was, my gold chain with a cameo on onyx ringed with tiny pearls, a gift from a spinster I often visited as a little girl. My sister wore it to school, broke and lost the circlet of pearls. Years later without asking me, Mother gave my wedding dress to someone who needed it.

Your mother had no borders with you.

She didn't value things. But she had a sense of quality and beauty. If she bought a suit, it would be the best, even if she had to wear it for years. Of a parishioner, Mother remarked to me after church, *I look better than she does in her full-length mink!* I admired her self-assurance. I admired her capacity for moral indignation. During the war, when I came home from our grade school basketball game at the YWCA in tears because they wouldn't let my friend Johanna swim in the pool after the game, Mother marched downtown, confronted them, and they opened the pool to the few black people in town.

Often you mention someone is rich. Why?

Many of the members of my father's church were wealthy; we were not. Both Mother and I felt the difference. I adored her, brought her pots of violets from the nursery with my baby-sitting quarters. Years later she told me I was the only one who gave her gifts, although once, after Dad died, her face flushed, wretched with tears, she beat her wrist watch, the sole gift he had given her late in his life. In profound grief, she told me she'd lost both her husband and her spiritual counselor. No one could fill that absence.

Mother cooked and sewed and knitted for me. She stood on a ladder alongside of Mrs. Lyfite, her once-a month housekeeping helper, rubbing pink putty to clean the sepia wallpaper with its scenes of English ladies in gardens with sculptures and fountains. It crumbled in dirty grains over her freckled arms and red hair, the Laughing Cavalier watching under his big black hat. Afternoons when I came home, she would be reading by the translucent green-curtained window and evenings she read long hours alone. In impulsive enthusiasm, I hugged her once. Startled, she didn't know how to respond.

She told me that she was happy as a child, though they were *poor as a church mouse.* The village had a store, no school, so weekdays she had to board in the nearest town. One summer we—she, my sister and brother and I—drove East to stay a month with Grandmother Bessie in upper New York state, where all of her family had lived for generations, most of them ministers who farmed. Grandmother, plump, warm, and cheerful, made blackberry jam and owned a Victrola on which I could listen to Caruso. Grandmother and Great-Grandmother made sure Mother went to Oberlin, with or without a dime.

Once in a dream, Mother came to me looking sorrowful, holding her pregnant belly. I felt guilt despite not knowing what I had done wrong. For years she let me to use oil paints and turpentine in her living room, listening over and over to the same records—Tchaikovsky, Rachmaninoff, Rossini—newspapers spread on the rug, under the easel. In grade school I took lessons in the home of a college professor who lived across town. In in high school I rode a commuter train on Saturdays to study at the Chicago Art Institute. I painted because I loved doing it and never pursued it as a profession. Before she died, she said with considerable disappointment, *You were the one I counted on to accomplish something*, which astounded me.

The Orange Suitcase

In a dream I drag my oversized, orange suede suitcase heading toward the Grand Hotel at Cabourg after a bus driver retrieved it from the luggage compartment. Reflecting on Proust, I realize he didn't write about dreams. I ponder memory as a source of illumination or potential illumination.

> A man wants to show me his art, a panel with a purple drawing on translucent paper appropriate for a church window. Suddenly, I realize my suitcase has disappeared. I replace it and fill the new luggage with everything I need, then it, too, is gone.

In France I can be nobody. I can lie in bed like a cat in summery air listening to Paris swifts at sunrise. Perhaps if I am drawing life with my own pen, its ink purple as a vein in my wrist, it won't matter if this luggage has been left behind.

The Edifice

The dying woman must begin to look upon the whole psyche as a grand, collective, religious, timeless edifice extending far beyond her personal life.

Jane Wheelwright

A man I met at the laundromat is driving me home in the wrong direction, claiming he's going toward St. Eustache. I know Paris and tell him to turn around and drive the opposite direction. Ignoring me, he drives into an empty stone and gravel lot. It is growing dark.

The organ of St. Eustache—how magnificent it is! That muted interior with prismatic light cast downward through the shadows, reminiscent of the church I prayed in when I was young. Once lost, can the power of worship ever be regained?

The driver listened to you, took you where you need to go even though it seems desolate.

Jane Wheelwright, her hair a soft white halo, is wearing a vivid spring green jacket embroidered in gold with Chinese characters.

Short, sprightly Jane was from infancy attuned to animals in their natural habitat. When Jerry and I arrived at the Wheelwright's retirement retreat on the family's Hollister Ranch, as I started to step out of the car, she cried out, *Don't disturb him!* A tumescent rattlesnake lay looped on the asphalt just beyond my foot. *They're cold blooded, they need the sun!*
Jane and Joe lived briefly in China and knew well Jung's appreciation of *The Golden Flower*.

Jerry holds out to me a yellow-green pencil with a white eraser.

The first time I met Jerry, I told him I no longer believed in God. He drew for me the sign for infinity ... *or God*, he said with a mischievous grin. His pencil—how symbolic—the word formed by stone, the graphite point. Green for the light of living nature and yellow for intuition, and most intriguing of all, the white eraser.

My daughter called to tell me she had been reading her journal, written in a brown empty notebook with special paper that had been Jerry's, when she came across a page on which he had written in his elegant, calligraphy-trained hand: We don't own the earth. I told my staff I was a theoblast. No one understood me.

> I am dealt a good hand for bridge, which included the ace and queen of diamonds. I ampleased because the ace could take the king. Just as I am about to bid, the woman to my right exposes her hand—an ace of hearts but all the rest low black cards—exclaiming it isn't worthwhile playing. I am defeated before I begin.

In a dream I lost my purse. What was in it? Billfold with cash, checks, coins, cosmetic case, hairbrush, pillbox (ceramic with flowers from the Parisian *quai*) cell phone, address book, calendar, papers, lists for groceries, things to buy, spiral notebook, two pens, keys, glasses (regular, sun, with cases).

What was not in it? My body, house, yard, car, computer, savings, investments, books, music, art, my poetry, family, friends, dreams, thoughts, and feelings, my past, my future, my spirit, my soul. The soul. The tree. The squirrel on a limb of the tree. The look in the eye of the squirrel on the limb of the tree.

I go to old man Jung and ask to talk to him. He looks at me with his penetrating eyes and intuitive mind, then says, I know. I tell him I don't know who I am. In my dreams I have lost my identity. He takes me out in his boat, gestures to be silent. We drift near shore. He leads me up the stairs inside Bollingen Tower. I have tried so hard, I say, but it all adds up to nothing. He has me show my hands, palms up.

All my life was written there.

At Risk

I brought home a little animal to butcher for a meal. The creature—warm, sensible of everything, of everyone—runs around exploring home. In my arms she trembles. I can't ... kill her.

A most appealing man arrives with a woman half my age.

At a psychology conference in the deep woods, a Hindu gives me his drumming CD. Suddenly, he's prone on top of me, then lifts himself up says, *SEX*, with a grin. A woman remarks, *He's not for you, you're not pretty*. In my mirror a Doris Duke—ravaged.

A mirror can catch me off guard. Great, time-worn groves of oceanside rock can move us with awe. Your own flesh and bone look unfamiliar, saggy, grim. Old-woman sex can crack a laugh in two. It's troublesome.

It's the negative in the female masculine troubles you most. Who told you that you were not pretty? That same voice says you can't publish, can't be public.

A girl, impulsively I asked my mother, *Am I pretty?* Distressed, she turned her face away. *Why do you ask me that!* An adolescent, I painted a self-portrait as accurately as I could using the dresser mirror. I painted myself in a blaze-red, off-shoulder dress. It shocked her. Vanity—a soul at risk.

Once Upon a Time

Standing in a coat of iron covering my body and head, a grid for my eyes, I can't open my mouth. I grow weak, collapse. Hands remove the headpiece.

I know the litany—don't laugh so loud, don't fight, don't be seen, don't speak. And even this was unspoken. It was the door my father slammed shut in my face whenever he came home to talk to Mother about his day's problems for "little pitchers have big ears."

A little girl asks me to hold her. I take her into my lap. Then she says, *Tell me a story.*

Once upon a time, a little girl lived with her sister and brother and parents, but they all went away except the mother, who didn't know how to hold a little girl. One day the little girl went to the tree and hugged it, but the tree said, *I can't hold you.* She climbed up the tree until she found a big, empty nest. She curled up inside it. A great bird came and told the girl to climb onto his back. He flew to a forest hut and let the girl down at the door of a white-haired woman who took her in and gave her cookies by the fire. The girl fell asleep. In the night, she awoke hearing scratching at the door. All alone, she opened the door. A great bear came in, but frightened by the fire, he rushed away. The next day the girl told the old woman about the bear. She gave the girl a ball of yarn to give to him. That night when the bear came, she held out the ball. He left carrying it in his mouth. The next morning, they followed the yarn to a cave. The old woman couldn't go inside and left. The girl went into the cave and discovered it wasn't a cave at all, it was a tunnel. When she walked through it, she came to a valley with leafy trees and flowers and streams. A king and queen lived there. The queen said they had lost a little girl and happily took the child into her arms.

DIES

Two exist within you—the king's daughter and the lonely child. You don't see who you really are.

A six-year-old was left at Day Care that closed. The child is shy and doesn't speak. The teacher, leaving, tells me the girl is *a little slow*, but in a few years, she will catch up. I want to call the police because I cannot imagine taking her with me. We are standing beside a darkened Chevron station. I can barely make out a sign: D I E S.

Someone in the dream said the name twice to me, a Latinate word for Fate.

Dies *dies solis*, day of the sun No! – D I E S

Black Onyx

A man gives me a cluster of three rings, one an extra-ordinary polished black onyx.

Last night my mood was black, burdened by angst—years of writing a waste, my analysis futile, my poetry, my life. But this black is exquisite, like a gemstone.

> An analyst worries about me, fears I will quit too soon. An eighty-year-old woman, a fellow analyst, enters, and they talk to me for an extra hour. He tells me not to worry about the time.

> A man helps me in underground water by using a white rocketlike pen.

The pen points to distance, outer space, masculine spirituality ... by way of words? Water underground, in the unconscious. In alchemy, white—not as innocence—appears after the nigredo, the descent into the dark unknown, in the process of psychological transformations ... a prediction?

Blood Everywhere

An enormous snake humping through liquefied mud between a man and me. *Get him out of here!* I cry. The man shrugs. Abruptly, the head emerges facing me. It's jaws open. I stab a stick into its throat. I think the snake will die but feel the fang's sting.

This snake bite signals that transformation is in process. It will lead to insight.

The doctor calls for Wozzeck because eye surgery reveals deeper surgery is necessary.

In the opera, Wozzeck did not see reality clearly, which led to tragedy, murder, and death.

I open the front door. Men burst into the house. One sets something on fire. I try to call the police. Silence on the line. A scream. Upstairs three men have cut off the breast of a young woman lying on a bed. Blood everywhere.

I have come for analysis of my dream. Three men are presenting their defense for charges against them. In another part of the complex, a smiling man says, *Go where they have an Amazon crocodile.* "That's the last thing I want to see!" Three men are in the room where I try to meditate before my session. One says, *That's passive-aggressive. No*, I think, and walk to a place where several people are naked. Am I naked under my shift? I step into sand and sink to my armpits. It's quicksand. I dare not move. Two men grip my hands and lift me out.

Sinking in quicksand signifies regression. All this is stirred up because of real fear.

Apples

In the movie *Prime Suspect*, the torture, mutilation, rape, and murder of a woman created in me a violent, visceral response. Many years ago, at a retreat at Big Sur, when shown a film in which a man was buried alive with excruciating, calculated, tedious attention, I rushed away from the others, gut-wrenchingly ill. In our women's circle, my shamanistic friend said that before she will expose herself to images, she asks herself, *How will it affect my immune system?*

> I am standing on a ladder handing down apples to a group of women.

Mary Cassatt casts a confident and natural light on feminine life. In my office I have hung a framed Cassatt print of a woman standing on a ladder handing down a fruit to another woman holding an infant.

Wondering how this dream can heal a wrong I can't even remember, I decided to see what the imagination might bring. Alone and in the dark, I closed my eyes and waited ...

Standing on a stony slope beside a huge boulder, I see below a vast desert plain and hear a creek flowing. I climb downward until I am immersed in a pinkish light. I can see nothing. A female voice says, *Step this way, you will be all right.* The light becomes a white cloud that circles upward like an inverse, lazy tornado. Before me women are gathered in a clearing of a deciduous forest. One with tan skin motions to follow her to its center. A fierce-looking, ancient matriarch asks harshly, *What do you want?* I answer that I don't know, I have come to a place in my life I do not understand. She says, *Look around at what they are doing.* Women are gardening, some are cooking, sweeping, sewing. It was clear: This is what you must do. No thinking. No plans. Just copy them. In time you will be shown a new way.

Large Red Signs

I dreamed of white-haired Robert Bly riding a huge phallus.

Get rid of him.

> A man leading a Catholic procession carries a red banner
> with gold insignia. A few of us who are opposed to them
> gather and enter the church, filling up the front and back
> rows, where I sit. The banner-carrier charges up to the
> chancel, he and his followers forcing their way through
> those of us still standing. Suddenly, a heavy-bodied naked
> woman strides up to the altar and proclaims, *The truth is
> ours!* A child joins her carrying a stuffed lamb.

~

Over and over in a dream I hear in blaring red: *AKRON,
AKRON*.

My second child, a son, was born in Akron. Cleaning cupboards,
I had fallen from a kitchen ladder and mistakenly thought my
waters had broken. Alone and uncertain, I called my physician
and was told to go to the hospital. I lay, unvisited, in the hospital
room. Nothing happened. Hours later, in the depths of night, I
was given Pitocin, a drug that creates immoderate, violent
contractions to induce labor. Later, because I could not tolerate
the pain, I was given twilight sleep, which keeps the patient awake
during labor and delivery, but she retains no memory of it. A year
or two later my husband, who was present as a first-year resident
at the delivery, told me that although I had not naturally begun
labor, the chief of ob-gyn wanted to demonstrate to his interns a
breach delivery. Potocin is used widely to induce labor when
necessary, but it can cause rupture of the uterus, asphyxiation of
the fetus, premature separation of the placenta, postpartum

hemorrhage and tetanus of the uterus. Fortunately, none of these possible disasters happened. Although both children's deliveries were breach, unlike my first birth which was dayslong and amazing, my son's birth had been taken from me, and that sweet bonding, that ecstasy, that *knowledge*.

AKRON – what is it in me that yields so blindly into the hands of a mere man as if he
were a god? Why didn't I speak up?

~

> I sit in a theater presenting a children's fairy tale called "Return to...." The play is long, and I leave. Returning, I find myself in a smaller, darker adult theater. Again, I leave and enter Macy's one-floor store. For a third time I return but I can't find the theater. I have lost my black purse. The lost-and-found is where? Outside I see a large red billboard:
> ### RETURN TO

While you were married to Jerry, you put aside what is unfinished, now you must go back.

Candlesticks

A bridge over a torrential river. A crisis. If I do not cross over, I will wander, lost, unseeing and unseen.

Packing to leave, I have little space left in my trunk. Piles won't fit. Three tall candlesticks, each in a different color. What can I do with them? A broom, a pail, a mop. An indignant cleaning lady says, *They're mine*! I stack items against the wall beside a red motorboat, distressed to leave so much. I have ten minutes to catch a train.

I've no idea where that train is heading but I want to catch it.

It's time I stopped playing the servant, one of a Jungian woman analyst's four female types, all defined in relation to men. Are the candlesticks symbols of the romantic? Am I to leave them as well?

Oh no. You inherited them from your mother. Take them with you. They are important feminine symbols, she says having migrated into my brain.

Psyche Is Timeless

Inside the house, an older man wants to reconnect with me by taking me on his boat. A boy interferes. The man and the boy have a talk behind closed doors. They return, the man almost in tears, the boy looking severe and worried but calm. As I am about accept the man, he puts the boat away, departs.

The boy is as he once was because the psyche is timeless. Here he interferes with your opportunity to relate to the man with a boat.

She explains that when I was a child, my male counterpart in the psyche acted out. Mother told me that at eight, after we moved, I threw temper tantrums. I don't know why. I do know that, after the move even to a more genial environment, I was aware that I spent most of my time alone. Before Mother died, she told me she never understood why I was disturbed, adding that when I began to paint, I improved.

My engineer friend explains the polarity of two spinning objects, how by magnetism one affects the other. What the boy does affects me, what I do affects the boy. All the inner figures and I are in this reciprocity.

A private pilot takes off, but the engine quits. I shut my eyes, certain we will crash, but he makes a soft landing on the beach. I think I could love him. He would be the other, some being deep in myself I could rely on.

The Performer

I dreamed an older performer wearing a vivid red outfit goes upstairs to remove her coat, then comes down in a matching red dress. She says I should be like her. I think she is bold, dramatic, and self-assured.

I dreamed an acrobat had a fight with her partner. When he climbed the rope to join her, she disengaged it at the top. He fell. I disapproved. Awake, I decided this she-me does not belong performing on a high-wire. And she's inflated, destructive. Or, I wondered, should he die?

I dreamed of a woman terrified, fleeing, but I knew there was nothing to fear.
I dreamed of Mr. Get-ahead jogging. How I dislike his self-promotion!
I dreamed Mr. Opera is my lover. I am among his major singers.

I dreamed a man puts his index finger to his mouth to silence me. As a child, I learned how not to speak—at the dinner table, in public, and definitely not in church. All my effort has been to defy that proscription. Of course, he might have meant to be still and listen to the dreams.

Fatal Disease

Night. An out-of-town bar filled with young people drinking, eating, some singing, some dancing, pointing upward with one then the other index finger. My dancing daughter, laughing, looks at me. I intuit she has told them this is my birthday. It is already 10:30. I am tired and want to go home but can't find my black purse. I go out to my car, thinking I left it inside it. My car isn't there. Walking down the road, I pass dirt front yards and worn-out-looking houses. I return. Everyone, even my daughter, and the cars are gone. Alone and frantic, I shout, *Everything is gone, my driver's license, my cards, my car with new tires!* Then I hear a resonant and low male voice: *Remember the fatal disease.* I cry out – and wake.

Each dream has as many aspects as a peacock's tail, but fundamentally this dream is about nearing eighty and not being centered.

Crossing a deep and treacherous ravine over a raging river, my feet sense the wood has become rope. I'm halfway, hanging onto two side ropes for balance as the bridge trembles and sways. I step one foot at a time, then pause to regain balance, steadying. A man's voice instructs, *Stand upright.* I do. The side ropes become firmer. I reach the edge, a shelf of land. To step onto it, I have to let go of the ropes. Frightened, I can't move.

FLOATING CHILD

What Jung does not say is that the child, so worthy of preservation as a representative of the human soul and its aliveness, can be permanently exiled by defensive processes and the anti-life forces that get established in the psyche after early childhood trauma. When this happens the soul goes into hiding, and its "urge to realize itself" may be all but extinguished.

Donald Kalsched

Derivation

A single bed, a silent meal, the mother's distracted *What do you want!* the unspoken mantra: wrong wrong wrong—from *rangr*: awry, unjust. Related to: to twist, to wring. Memory a distorting mirror. How to perceive the past clearly?

Your mother did not give the approval the child needs.

She loved me, told me she wanted me, told me my father didn't, his reason her pleurisy (though healed). The reason never sounded the reason and upset me, though I couldn't grasp why. However, it *was* the peak of the Great Depression of which as a young child I had no notion.

Night. I go up steps to the entry of a large unlit house. Its carved, heavy double doors have two oversized doorknobs which I cannot turn. No one answers my knocking. Barely within my reach is a knocker with a lion face. With both hands I slam it. The doors open. It is dim inside. Uneasy but compelled, I enter, call out. No one comes. Then, in the shadows, I see my mother as she looked when I was a child, graceful, well-formed. She asks why I have come. I say I thought I was going through death's door. *You did. What do you want of me?* I say I want her to love me. *I did love you.* I want to feel held. Backing into the shadows she says, *I cannot.* Then I am outside, alone, held in the sensation of endless loss.

~

Walking through the woods I come to a clearing. A man stands before an easel holding a white board. On it he had drawn in black outline a large eye with lines rayed from it. He sends a little child into the forest to get something. I worry what might happen to her, but the child does not seem afraid.

The eye of God? A sun god? The child seems fearless. Perhaps she's used to it. For years I played alone in the vacant church while my father was occupied.

What you don't see is that the father isn't caring for the child. The child doesn't understand fear and should not have been sent into the forest alone.

63

What the Body Knows

A dear friend, whom I have known for years, was visiting for a week. We had a terrible row. As it escalated, I became unable to speak. His anger felt huge. Shaken and nauseated, I fled into my bedroom, locked the door. He shouted outside of it. Eventually, he left. I lay on my bed, curled into a fetal position, trembling and icy cold. My whole body began to shudder in waves of upheaval. The wetness of tears. Short shallow panting. My mind opaque. No sensation of time. It began to subside, then resumed with less force. Quiet. I lay motionless, enervated. He returned, knocked, softly pleaded with me to let him in, telling me he has horrible dreams if he goes to sleep without working through the problem. I let him in. We talked, and talked, and at the end hugged each other, affectionately.

Abreaction.

I never had this happen before.

It could happen because you knew you could trust him. He would never harm you.

Variations of this trauma have appeared in dreams. In my fifties, my now-deceased analyst sent me to a body therapist to try to understand why I was having nightmares at the same time as I was very happy in my marriage, my poetry writing, and my professional life. One day she put pressure on the coin-sized area of my back where spasms occur beside a thumb-sized deformation of my spine. I became overwhelmed with revulsion. Nauseated, I got myself home, driving as if I were feeble, then showered, and then fell into a heavy, midday sleep. My analyst and I gradually decided then that when I was little, an adult male had attacked me. I could remember only lying curled up on a wood floor, the shoes—a man's black lace shoes, the smell of damp wool as if in a cloak room. I think of it now and then when my back goes into spasms.

The Red Cloak

In an old two-story house in the middle of nowhere, lonely as a Hopper painting, I go around locking every door, every window. I want to be sure the woodshed door is locked but I am reluctant to go outside to check it.

Returning to a house where I left some of my belongings, I find that the couple inhabiting it have deranged and spilled out my things. My beautiful old vanity has been blocked by an ugly, unfinished piece of furniture. A tall man has forced himself on women in the house and roams around naked. Avoiding him, I find a baby in a bassinet. She and the bedding are soaked. I change her and replace the sheets. He seems responsible for her neglect. I see to it that the baby will be taken care of. Intending to leave, I gather up what is mine.

The chilling loneliness in childhood is still present in your psyche, and the fear. The roving man is rapacious. The movement through it begins when you care for the infant and prepare to leave with what belongs to you.

I am lowering a coffin into a grave. It's but too heavy. A man begins to help.

Leaving the guest house, I cross ground flat as a lake going toward the far shore lit up by a hotel. The sky clouds. The hotel is farther away than I had expected. When I arrive, the lights have gone out, the hotel is closed. On the long way back, everything is pitch dark, but the front entry is lit. I can see the double doors. To enter I will have to wake up mother from her deep sleep.

Whom was I trying to bury? How do you wake up the dead? Or why? My mother resides in death. For a month, unable to shake free of this dream experience, I traveled with my daughter—Rome, Naples, Sicily. Among a maze of images, a fountain with water pouring from the gaping jaws of a snake startled me. Out of death's jaws flows the water of life?

> I am climbing up to the top of a snow-covered slope with my daughter. She warns me to be careful. I begin to slide down and down. I slide into a wood building. I try to find my way back but I am standing in a tourist shopping center. I worry that my daughter must be panicking and I don't know how to get back to her. I am hungry but have nothing to eat. An old man offers me a red cloak.

I was falling apart! The tinnitus louder and piercing. My pinky finger broken from a fall that will take months to heal. Vertigo. Fatigue. Lousy circulation, crazy leg cramps at night. My reading glasses wrong, my third pair of sunglasses lost. My spelling gone awry. My word slippage worse. Past achievements, past publication meant nothing to me. I was troubled over ways I had failed those I loved most. My daughter's efforts to protect me can't prevent the hazards of age. Even my dreams depressed me. How could a red cloak change anything?

Paper Bag

I put fragments of a plot on the blackboard to express the idea that I had the ability to contain in myself the Powers—FRBO (For Rent By Owner) stood for it. I had to get rid of this quickly, or it would explode and destroy the world. I sent it into a goat that would be killed and eaten.

Here you have a sense of being invested by the Self with power, but the power of your rage has frightened you. You send it into a scapegoat and sacrifice your own instincts.

My grandson and I had an encounter over the dishes he left in the sink, *my sink*. I had a disagreement with my daughter and felt her statements distorted my position, but I could not defend myself. A bitter, angry, self-obsessed person in our reading group could not stop talking, and I was unable to halt or divert her. One of our members called wanting me to do something. I thought that the only power I had was to feel frustrated. Only later did I work it out with the woman in a good way.

A man takes me to a conelike volcano surrounded by a lake. Blue-purple wavelets touch my feet.

You were angry.

Frustrated. Anger in my parents' house was not permitted. My fatherless father was adamant, having been repeatedly abused by his oldest brother who drove him at twelve or thirteen off the family's sugar-beet farm with a pitchfork. Even when I asked my first husband for a divorce, I was not angry.

You were angry, at him, at your grandson, at your daughter, at the bitter narcissistic woman.

My granddaughter stands outside a complex, saying, *Awesome!* I see a squirrel coming down the trunk of a large tree with a paper bag over its head. Reaching the ground, it turns its head this way and that, not knowing or even smelling, completely vulnerable. I feel sorry for the small creature but can't figure out how to cut the sack off. I hear men laughing. Their mockery makes me furious.

To get outside this complex the way your granddaughter was is crucial. Only then can you see clearly and defend your perceptions and feelings.

Tears

I ride the elevator down with a small greenish man.

The elflike green man of folklore has nature's wisdom, also he's magic.

> I'm standing before double doors with a friend. Cheerfully announces to everyone that the hosts are serving a meal along with the program. Then the doors shut, leaving me outside.

> My friend enters a bar where men are gambling.

These dreams *expose unconscious competitive animus. You have conflict with this woman because she mirrors an aspect of your own shadow.*

We arranged to lunch together. She began combative. This time, aware of my own ego needs and my desire to remain friends, I didn't join battle. I stayed related, and soon so was she. We both felt the change and parted with a warm embrace.

Because you are clearer about who you are, you can stay more bordered. Staying bordered makes it possible not to succumb to the unconscious of another person.

> At the same friend's house, I see flying insects or birds hovering over her desk. I say how pretty and multicolored they are. She is serving a special cake to the others while I go into the kitchen to make a phone call.

> I am pregnant and don't know what to do with my condition.

> My grandson and Jerry are bent over a workbench making something together.

Unaccountably moved by this dream, tears came into my eyes. I rarely cry.

Floating Child

A dead child is floating in a circular pool. Two orange tablets are dissolving in the water. Devastated, I lie enervated on a couch. A young man makes acidic wise-cracks. I suspect he caused the child's death but suppress my anger because I can't prove it. I want the authorities to arrive before the tablets dissolve completely so they can test for acid.

A man shows me how to mix white grit like ground gypsum into the solution to layer, like gesso, onto the canvas before I paint.

These dreams seemed to me to reference alchemy and art. Frustrated, I asked my analyst why didn't she amplify them that way?

It's the grit of life itself we're working on—that's an art, isn't it?

The next day in a room with others, a friend abrasively contradicted me. Feeling attacked, I said no more, but I felt our friendship was failing, which led to a distressed, awake night.

You can stay really related by not hitting back only if you don't withdraw. You must not just go silent. It will help if you can stay with those who value you. More importantly, you must learn to feel compassion for yourself when a situation like this one occurs.

Having compassion for myself hovered between incomprehensible and ludicrous. The word itself means to feel "with" someone else. With someone else, intending to be helpful, I commented about his actions. He took offence, turned hostile, and I felt the power of his anger, then dreamed I was inside an alligator's mouth.

Suicidal Woman

Returning to the house in which I lived while in grade school, I go to the toilet. When I turn to flush, a man is watching me. He says, *I did not believe you would return where you had murdered someone.*

Guilty! without knowing why.

Look at it this way: This figure is a phenomenon of the psyche itself that protected you by blocking the memory of trauma. Now he attacks by making you feel guilty of an unforgivable act to prevent you from experiencing the reality and the actual suffering of what happened to you as a child. Often your dreams show the dark side of your family but that does not mean the man who assaulted you was your father. Yet something real happened in that bathroom.

A friend of mine is being gang-raped. Afraid, I am trying to stay invisible. Later her husband comes, and she doesn't want him around. He gets aggressive. There is conflict between them.

This woman was gang-raped when she was young, and she resented the fact that her father had not protected her. Here, I am merely the observer.

Porous as you are, what happens to others happens in your psyche. This is a valuable trait, not a fault; it enables empathy, but it also increases vulnerability. Her trauma comes too close to your own, unacknowledged suffering.

In a car with my paintings in the backseat, the woman driving stops dead at the cliff-edge. It is so precarious I am afraid that if we try to get out, the car will tip over the cliff, and all my paintings will be destroyed.

Who is she? Driving recklessly with my paintings, my poetry ... my life? The sense of jeopardy was so keen I couldn't deny the disturbing sense of having given over my fate unconsciously to another.

Loss of Soul

H, drunk, drives us into a ditch

Shortly after her second mastectomy, H was robbed, brutally hurt and raped by a thug who broke into her apartment, leaving her so traumatized she could no longer live in her own home.

> An enormous black bull has been let outside. I am angry because I will have to go get him, and that will be difficult.

Both dreams are about trauma and its effects, an inner dynamic of victim and perpetrator. You have been unaware of the bull with his powerful instinctive aggression; however, you have become responsible for controlling him—no easy task.

> A woman examining my vagina excises a small section. I feel the quick cut. She tells me it was cancer. She has removed it. Then an older man cuts deeper, removing four or five more cancerous pieces.

Metaphorically cancer growing in the vagina is caused by assaults on feminine nature, its instinctual quality, its relatedness. Psychic cancer is deep and lethal.

> A man puts two heavy mercury balls into my palms to hold out, keeping them and myself in balance.

Mercury is dangerous, fatal.

Jung wrote that Mercurius is the primordial light-bringer, the light of nature, the light of the moon. He contains all opposites, both material and spiritual, and therefore symbolizes wholeness, especially the whole process of alchemical transformations.

The Wand

A conflict. Dictatorial rancor. I hold out a stick to create harmony. A seven-year-old girl steps out of fog, takes my hand and guides me to porch steps. A fair woman with shoulder-length hair, wearing a soft, beige garment, greets us. Bewildered, I ask, *Where am I?* She says, *You are in life and you are also here with us.* She points to my stick and wordlessly lets me know I have a magical wand in life, have had it since I was a child. She seems to be a godmother, real but not human.

In a dream I heard: *The vibrations from the image are sent by an angel.*

White Horse

From my window a white horse lying on the ground a man poised to shoot.

This high-spirited animal is in you. You think if you just achieve something more than you have already done, others will give you what you want but they won't. Whatever you accomplish will never be enough. The horse has the instinct to run, not race.

My hand – my writing hand! A man is going to cut it. At my distress he offers anesthesia. Another is going to do cutting. A third man says he used a needle to remove a node in core of my palm.

These figures are progressively less brutal but still cutting. Judging your creative work and yourself from their collective point of view harms you.

Behind the Façade

My mother is in the bedroom. I pick up a skinny little dog that had been left outside.

Driving with my mother sitting so close to me, I can't steer. The car careens toward a concrete abutment. Desperately, I swerve to the right, brake—yelling *Move!* but she seems deaf.

The eternal psyche holds the child who went without emotional connection with the mother who listened but could not hear.

In the house of a wealthy family I knew as a child, guests are eating at a long table, but the meal isn't real. I go to the bathroom in the center of the house. Hidden behind rich ebony panels I discover a dirty sink and tub. I begin to clean them when two young sisters enter. They mentioned Mary, their mother. *You mean she's dead?* I ask. *She died a month ago.* She'd fallen in the snow, but her death had not been announced because everyone was waiting to hear if she'd won the skiing contest, they explain. I'm appalled. The older sister told me she hadn't decided which of the famous colleges she would attend, and the younger one put into my hand a church made of raspberry sugar candy, warning me to hold it carefully just as it broke apart. Mary's husband had no one to care for him. He needed mercury to stay alive, he needed to go to France. I leave, but at the black wrought iron gate, I realize I have forgotten my keys, watch and purse. Retrieving them, I leave knowing I will never return.

This is a major dream. In this house of the wealthy, there is no real nourishment. Behind the façade of panels at the center is their shadow you try to clean up. The woman's achievement and ambition led only to death. This couple were secular parent substitutes for you, but in their house the sacred like candy falls apart, not possessing the great spiritual quality of the cathedrals of France you love. The husband lacks mercury; that is Mercurius, contact with the gods. What has changed is that you remembered and retrieved what is most valuable—the keys to your house, your car, your access to what can sustain you, your relationship to time, your identity and more. You left with your ego intact.

The Blind Seer

Inside a barnlike garage, a great black bear lumbers toward me. I press the garage door switch, closing it just in time. Laborers are constructing a theater stage with upper levels previously intended for a private residence. A gang of young people invades my house. With effort I get them to leave.

Once *SUNDERED* was published, I had to arrange readings, a task I find onerous. When the book arrived, I was moved by my daughter's cover image from her painting "Premonition of Jerry's Death." Rereading the poetry after all these years (how long? thirteen since I wrote it?) I was surprised. I found it powerful, and it hardly seemed composed by me. Some other had voice had spoken.

In a lecture-reading about the dark imagination, a listener asked, *How did you find the courage to expose your own darkness to the world?* Another listener remarked that only Jungians would understand these poems. Then, weeping, an elderly woman told of her night terrors and asked how she could end them. I answered, *Work with them*, but she shook her head, slumping down, distraught.

An emaciated old man had nothing to eat.

It is good not to feed this old man because he represents rigidity, as opposed to courage, change, growth.

A man with indents for eyes and a pockmarked face takes my hand. I let him hold it awhile, and then he presses it against his heart, saying, *You will be a poet.*

He is a version of the blind seer Teiresias. It raises the question, what kind of a poet will you become?

Demeter

My toddler heads toward the edge of a roof. I plunge to save her. We fall, but I protect her with my body.

Traveling, my daughter and I go in different directions; then I hear her scream.

Like Demeter you could not protect her, or yourself. Both dreams express the woman's experience in our world and a mother's attempt to prevent harm. It is archetypal.

Body and Psyche, Underground

As has been happening with increasing frequency, my back went into spasm.

> Asleep on a bench at the storefront end of a deli and liquor store, I wake seeing a dark-haired, heavy-set man at the back door who disappears down basement stairs. Suddenly, a big-bosomed, middle-aged, mean-looking, red-headed woman grabs my arm. She threatens to call the police. I struggle to get free. She grows large, strong, and terrifying. I submit, plead with her, telling her I am in pain. Gradually, she resumes her original form. A young man comes, tells her, *Let her go, she has done no harm.* He takes me to the back door. As I am leaving, he offers me fruit to eat. Recalling Persephone in Hades, I decline. Then he offers a veggie wrap. I bite into it just as I walk toward the door. As I pass the basement stairs, I feel cold air rising. It is pitch dark below.

This narrative offers multiple amplifications. You dream it as the girl who experienced it and as an adult witness. The woman didn't want you to see her husband who went below. Why? What were they concealing? The dream repeats the trauma, where you were helpless, where it went underground. It was and is disturbing.

> In the center of an old European town, I walk past a church and down a long flight of stone steps. I walk out of town on a dirt road through a field. Two boys are beating a snake to death on a stone. They break the back of a small animal, perhaps a dog. One boy gets on it to ride. The animal looks at me with suffering eyes across an abysm I cannot cross.

I woke in despair. The cruelty felt medieval. The snake, classic symbol of transformation, of healing, ancient as Asclepius and the medical caduceus . . . What herald of malignancy would display this sadistic viciousness? Why must I, who cannot prevent it, witness it?

On Sin

I hear a man outside my house saying, *It's sinful, what you are doing is sinful.* He has been released from a mental hospital. Even though I know I am dreaming, know he is crazy, a religious fanatic, I close and lock my window, pull the drapes closed.

The insane, demonic, actively destructive man is a presence in your psyche. Something happened to punish you.

In a small dimly lit church which I had attended years before, the preacher, after his sermon, goes behind a screen. I am crying. A young girl leaps up and prances around on a stage in a short skirt without underpants. Her father stands at the back of the church looking at her with disapproval, then disappears. A crude stranger tries to force her to go with him; she fights him. As the congregation leaves, I go to her. She tells me the man wants to slit her throat. I sense some forbidding presence watching us. In the church kitchen, I ask her if I can find underpants for her. *No! I don't like them!* she declares, and I realize she is just a child.

My father would have disapproved of the sexy little girl's jubilant behavior, but, if he could, he would have protected her from the crude man. Always, at the end of the service, he stood at the back of the sanctuary, black-robed arms raised to give the blessing in his deep, resonant voice:

> May the Lord bless you and keep you. May the Lord shine his face upon you
> and be gracious unto you. May the Lord lift up his countenance upon you
> and give you peace.

The blessing moved me deeply.

Sun Glasses

Midnight. I bent over to remove a spider from the empty bathtub. Suddenly dizzy, I fell in. No one heard my scream. Third hard fall in three years; the last one occurred when I was rushing up the stairs trying to keep up with my six-foot, marathon-enthusiast grandson. Yesterday I drove over my new sunglasses. I seem unable to attend to what I am doing.

The falls you've had! What is distracting you? Why are you in a hurry?

It never goes away—an urgency. I hurry, and something gets lost, broken, damaged.

> Smiling, my friend gives me a letter telling me how much he enjoyed being with me. Hurrying down high stone steps, I realize I'd forgotten something. I go back up then rush down again, this time carrying my small dog and house keys. By the time I get to my door, it's dark. I drop my keys. Still holding the dog, I bend over to pick them up. A man behind me hits the back of my head with a heavy object.

All is warm and friendly with your male friend, then abruptly there is darkness and violence. She looked at me the way at certain moments Jerry did—as if he were talking to someone else in my head.

> On a large estate, I have taken a seat in a chapel for a lecture. A man pushes until I have only part of a seat, so I leave. I lose a pair of my glasses, then break one lens of the pair I am wearing. I put on my sunglasses, but they are too dark. Outside there has been a flood. The ground slants into water, and walking is slippery. I am frightened because I am alone and don't know where to go.

What the Snake Knew

A snake glides down a hallway and slides into my room. Stock-still, my little dog watches. I pick her up, fearing she will be attacked. The snake rears facing me with a weird smile. A voice says, *You can't befriend a rattlesnake.*

This voice is wise. You trust too much. You want everyone to like you, and that's dangerous.

The snake indicates, *follow him.* Ignoring a warning voice, I do, carrying my little white dog. We walk into a blinding light. Something forces down on my head a crown of iron thorns. Despite the pain, I continue walking, seeing nothing, feeling the warmth of the dog's body. Then the brilliance fades. Moving past vague, the snake slithers toward a massive tree with bright globes in its branches. The snake winds around the trunk, its head disappearing into the leaves. I let the dog down, and she disappears into light. Hearing her furious barking, I follow her and come to a twilight realm. Before me stands a majestic figure wearing a dark moss-green mask and robe, slightly parted. Nothing but pitch-black inside. She says, *I am death.*

A stabbing pain circled my head. I was terrified.

Dark Place

I'm told to write a poem about death. Instead, I paint on paper an emerald vase with holes through which one can see a dark interior. Above it I print DEATH, then wonder if I should print it at an angle across the vase as if crossing off the vase itself. Then I think not.

My writing hand was diagnosed with an old man's disorder— Dupuytren's Contraction Disease, which is genetic, progressive, and incurable. The fingers contract, making a claw. They force us, these forces, don't they? An immaculate knowing. Already nearing the end.

The Fisherman

A man I had known and desired arrives with his partner and two children. I give them food, shelter. The attraction between us has never abated. Aware, his hippie woman stays in shadows, preventing us from intimacy. Standing on high ground, I know I must descend to cross the river at the bridge below. The way down has many streams, and it's too steep for a woman and her children. We will have to backtrack, take the long way around the hilltop to descend to the bridge. Finally, alone together, he and I kiss.

You connect with the man only after you take care of the woman and the children; that is, after you take the long difficult descent and integrate the feminine.

We return to the house we own but have rented. The male tenant left the hot tub uncleaned and damaged. I drain it and begin repairs when I see far out an enormous whaleback of water heaving toward shore. The ocean has risen hundreds of feet. A few people reach the ashore, including a weathered, ancient-looking man standing up in an old-fashioned fishing boat. I did not know how to save the children.

You worry too much about others. It overwhelms you. You are worried about the country, the world, the future. You are worried about your family and dramatize their life issues and fears. They are fine. The child in you is anxious, and you need to take care of her, not them. Aging makes us all vulnerable, but extreme anxiety is from childhood. The old man with his fishing boat is a potent spiritual figure, a symbol of drawing sustenance from the sea of the unconscious.

Stuck

An enemy is after me, a killer. Hastily, I thrust my possessions under a sheaf of papers, afraid he can easily discover them. A small caged dog looks at me sorrowfully.

Instincts are caged when the killer takes over. Soul-destroying judgments over what you write, what you think, what you say—these are his.

A man and I are standing below houses built on the hilltop, their yards adjacent with no way of descent. A hellish steam rises from ice and snow covering rocks on which we stand.

Rock and ice, a hard place—you are stuck. This animus isn't helpful.

A chauffer is driving. I sit beside him restrained in handcuffs. I long to have rider in the back seat touch my crotch, but she is caressing another woman.

His restraint is sadistic because it provokes and simultaneously thwarts the desire to touch and be touched by the feminine.

All You Need

A man gives me a vase—ball-shaped base, neck narrow, mouth flared like a chemistry lab flask. He stretches plastic wrap over the lip, saying, *This is all you need.*

One of the first dreams I learned to recall, forty-six years ago, pictured myself as a girl sanding, holding a vase between my father and myself. It slipped from my hands, breaking into a thousand pieces. As if privy to knowledge beyond her years, she knew something horrific had happened.

The vase is a feminine container for the self, for the water of life, for the soul.

At a central island in a spacious kitchen, my friend sits rolling gibbous eyes as if something is wrong with her. On the island is a bone china bowl, gold-rimmed with a delicate grapevine pattern. She wants it, but I did not want to give it to her. Turning to the stove, I flip the overhead vent light switch. Oddly, the inside of the oven lights up.

Magic? Because I refused her envy?

This woman carries a shadowy aspect of you. Her body suffers because she is controlled by unconscious forces. She is needy and a big problem for you.

The Bolero Suit

In a rambling house on the periphery of a European village, I am alone, though living with my family and others. I open a door to an unlit, abandoned room with tools and a potsherd of discarded objects. Another door leads to an empty room with a partial swinging doorframe that exposes the outside.

I am trying to keep the family together. My brother is hungry. I find a restaurant where I can see the red outline of one of the Camargo Foundation buildings in Cassis, France. I find a wood table where we could all sit, and I ask the owner what her aged mother would cook for us. My brother wants fruit. She says I would have to go to the market for that. I say I will. Then she adds, you will have to woo the old woman. I answer, I will do that too.

Alone in your family's house, the door you opened led you outside yourself. In that matrix, you became the one who took care of others. This time the old wise woman will cook for you, will give you what you need—if you woo her, that is.

I am wearing a blood-orange red outfit like my bolero suit.

That was my favorite outfit, which I saved for special occasions. Without asking, Mother gave it to my sister, who was away at Shimer, a private high school and college in Waukegan, an opportunity I would have loved but was denied because as a good student I "didn't need it." I never saw the suit again.

Now you are wearing it—blood red! The vitality and passion that belong to you.

The Hose

A purposeful man takes me to a barnlike space where two brawny creatures lie asleep on a dirt floor. Tied by a rope, a German shepherd strains toward me. I reach my hand out toward his head. My guide says, *Don't touch him!* Then he points—nearby—the large, raw-looking penis of the sleeping animal. As if nudged, his eyelids slightly open.

It smolders, insuppressible. You cannot assimilate what you do not see.

A man spraying a plant beckons me. Hesitantly, I go to him. Standing behind me, he puts his arms around me, helping me hold the hose. We have three plants to water.

Of course, it's sexual, but consider the contrast between the two dreams. In the second, the man is helping you to use masculine sexual energy to provide what life must have to grow and thrive.

Icon

I enter a dilapidated, abandoned chapel where a man shows me a wood carving of a rayed sun with a woman's face. We will restore it, clean and repaint the gold leaf and fern green.

In this chapel, where once your religious feeling was abandoned, the woman in the sun is being restored. She is connected to the sun god, able to be allied with male spiritual energy. Gilded, earth-connected, she is holy, strong, warm. Hold on to this in yourself. It shines through you when you are not obstructed by negative, self-denigrating thoughts.

Coming Down

Piloting a private plane, I have strayed over the ocean. A man warns me, *Get back*. I swerve overland at a thousand feet, anxious, not knowing where I am. The land is flat and green and split by a road with a yellow centerline. Flying low above it, I come to crossroads.

My small dog runs down stone steps toward the water. Afraid for her, I follow. At the base of the steps stands a red-haired, queenly woman wearing an eighteenth-century gown, a white puddle under her arm. She holds a globe.

The century that commences oceanic journeys and discovery. Feet firmly on the ground, the queen stands poised in her own authority.

The Waterfall

A disheveled man with an ugly face broke into my house, stole my medical alert that hung by my bed. The phone line has been cut. Dogs are barking ferociously behind the fence.

This intruder frightened me, he felt like Death—an immanent violent death.

I want to own the upper left apartment of a square four-unit building.

What I want is a response to the first dream. An upper room for safety, a spiritual space in a grounded, four-square, psychological structure.

Looking out a bus window, I see an immense waterfall over a granite cliff face, tons and tons of water thundering into the lake below. I wanted the others to look, to see.

The waterfall—its immense energy flows through you.

The Office

Entering my analyst's house, I walk through dim, shadowy rooms. I sit holding a worrisome, indecipherable dream. She's hard to talk to, as if her mind's elsewhere. Her dog pesters me, as if he wants to get into my lap. Responding to something, I ask if she had had anything to eat. *No*, she answers. *Eat*, I say. She begins to chew on something. Another woman enters. I go into an adjacent room. It's been two hours. Distraught, I decide to leave.

Does my analysis feed her needs rather than mine? The dog looked like the frantic, neglected stray I'd adopted at some cost, then had to return because his need for attention was maddening. She listened to the dream, waited.

In here you can say anything.

"When you said, *I like you*, nothing changed between us. All that's been dredged up, all that flotsam and jetsam of my life. ... Nothing has been transformed. You told me I need to accept myself. How in the midst of this sludge?"

You can't do that until you learn how to be loving toward yourself. We need to stay together, to stay where the analysis can get deeper.

The Obsidian Mirror

My artistic friend and I have lost our way on a forest road. We stop at a wood lodging. Inside, men wearing uniforms and insignia are dismissive of our questions. To get assistance from one man, I lie, saying my son was ten—implying he might join them, but he has no directions to offer. We drive on. It becomes misty. Ahead, the mountain peaks are covered with snow. When we come to another house, the weather has worsened. On the front porch water drips through holes in an awning. The woman inside doesn't know what direction we should take but suggests we dial 114 on the car radio. As we drive, the road ahead disintegrates.

This isn't a dark dream; it's promising. After you lie to the man, you come to a woman who can live in the forest alone. The woman's numbers are symbolic of both the feminine and wholeness. In life, this friend with you is very grounded in reality. She's a fine extrovert and healthily ambitious.

I was talking to a friend about a performance, telling her to play the major part.

"I'm dissembling, really thinking I should play the major part. It's about inflation, narcissism!"

You're not narcissistic! You need more of it!

The Heart

I watch the furrowed hands of an elderly spinster pouring tea. Stirring honey into my demitasse, she says, *Look around. Do you recognize where you are?* Tall windows with velvet, burgundy drapes. Then I remember— she is the woman I visited who lived in the big house at the end of the block, the one who gave me a gold necklace chain with a cameo of a lady's silhouette on black onyx encircled by little pearls. *You used to visit; you were very talkative. You came often. Then something happened, I never knew what. You never came again. I have something for you.* Leaning forward, she hands me a small gilded chest embedded with tiny gems. *Open it.* Lifting the lid, I see a ruby the shape of a heart, a pulsing heart. She closes the lid and whispers, *Keep it, always. Whenever you feel lonely, open it.*

GNOSIS

...a perception that wells up from the inner experience, a type of perception that is at the same time a vital experience.

C. G. Jung

Oneiric Vision

Standing beside me as we watch an eclipse of the sun, my beloved puts his arm around me. At the moment of totality, at the diamond effect, we hold hands.

In my daughter-in-law's kitchen I am helping fix breakfast when my son calls me into the adjoining room. Gesturing toward the window, he exclaims. *Look!* Just above the trees hovers an immense sphere—huge, glittering like a moon or planet of diamond chips, silver and gold.

Keep these, hold them. Your eyes have such a light!

Intruders

Late in the day strangers from a religious sect boldly enter my house and begin taking everything, even a high-hanging tapestry, my clothes, my writings, Jerry's ties, his cherished art from all over the world. In the darkness, I walk down our long driveway, passing workers digging up our plants and burying them in concrete. Coming a multileveled apartment complex, I climb outside steps looking for our elderly friends. No one answers the knocker at their door. I am afraid they might be dead inside. I continue to the roof, where I gaze down into three empty shells under construction. I am alone and have nowhere to go.

Shaking, I awoke, my skull hurting, the ringing in my ears harsh. I felt helpless, confused, afraid I was being warned of imminent death.

This is about death, death as transition. The end of the old way. The new apartments on the upper floor, however, are unfinished.

A tall woman in tan leather with a wolflike dog enters my apartment, its door lock broken. Ignoring me, she begins to search for something. Frightened, I try to call out *help* but my voice is uncannily weak. Three men come. I ask one to call 911. Police arrive. Someone says they are going to excavate under the house.

I fitted a square board into the ledge framing a concrete opening. Something is buried below.

After you lost Jerry, you were thrown back into the original complex, which has not yet been resolved. The aggressive masculine is still buried and active in the unconscious.

Grand Old Chestnut Grove

An admired, widely loved poet and I are lounging in bed. He talks about retirement and his wife. I wonder if he intends to stay with her. He says yes but he will also stay with me. She brings him a *Croque Monsieur* made in my kitchen.

He is a very public man. I'm not like him, nor do I wish to be. To retire, for him and for me, is age-appropriate. Whatever is achieved will never be enough for his ambitious wife. Why is she here in my psyche?

She's shadow, feeding him rich food, which isn't good for him at his age. He is potential, a creative animus.

I am on a street with ochre stone apartment buildings fronted by a row of dormant trees reminiscent of an *arrondissement* in the Paris I love. I stand before an entry holding a beautiful, handmade bowl like the one I bought for myself at a grand old chestnut grove in France. In it lay my checkbook and a coiled-up cord, which I stretched out with both hands.

You need to stretch, to widen your responses. When you get contracted, you react impulsively, giving too much to others. It's costly.

Somber Offering

The poet sitting to my right at the dinner table says something foolish. *It's all right*, I say, *I do that myself.* He glares at me as if to say, *How dare you compare yourself to me?* My dog poops on the rug, then eats it.

He's denigrating. The dog eats her own excrement, turning it inward as if what is wrong is her fault. You still need to grasp fully that, as a child, you longed to be seen and valued. Think of your childhood memories!

That winter night at the wealthy lawyer's home? The new sweaters his wife bought for my sister and me. That evening while others talked below, I stayed on the stairs that led up to the bedrooms, hugging my sweater's honey-beige softness. How amazed I was, how comforted!

That parishioner who stopped in to visit? When she said she wanted to take me home, I packed my toy suitcase and waited in the entry. Later, telling me the story I had forgotten, Mother laughed.

Why do I have to go back to childhood? It's frustrating and humiliating at my age.

This neglect has been in you from the beginning. You repressed it, put it aside, survived because you were by nature high-spirited. Survived, but at great cost. You don't have to depend on that anymore.

She gave me a somber look.

Conundrum

A boy about ten standing at the edge of a canyon river's turquoise pool wants to dive in. I don't know what the darker areas hold or where the river flows. I warn him it is dangerous. He dives in anyway.

This boy was me—his impetuousness, his fearless love of water.

My car has been parked in the dark after a rainfall. Two men standing by another car are having a dispute. One objects, *You didn't do what I asked you to do!* When I try to start my car, the wheels spin in mud. I try to rock it free; it tips over on its side. When I get out of the driver's seat, the men have gone. I tip the car back up myself and start it. Slowly, the wheels grip. I drive onto the road.

Why didn't you ask the men to help? You think you can handle anything, even righting the car, then you get sick. That strong spirit in you needs to be in balance with your human limits.

I have just finished a large load of laundry. Many people congregate in my house. One of them asks if she can lie down on my bed. She's freezing. I cover her with one of the extra-large bath towels I have just laundered. Another person comes, and then another.

The dream reminded me of a movie made in India in which a man feeds someone who comes to the door hungry, then another, then several, then over the hill comes a multitude.

Psyche's task in the underworld. She must contain her compassion and not yield to the piteous cries of others. If she does, she will never return to the world of the living.

Numinous Head

A man's torso and beautiful head with classical Greek features, eyes closed, brow encircled by a platinum band wound by a circlet of white roses. He wears a peaked hat. Above it—a quick flicker of fire.

Go further with this; it's potent.

As I have done occasionally in times of confusion or distress or incomprehension, I sat in a dark room, hands in my lap, palms open, and waited. I tried to keep the image in my mind:

His eyelids flash open, his glance intense, fiery, then they shut. Standing in a prism, as if in a cathedral of stained glass, I hear an organ playing a Bach fugue with passion and resonance. A king and queen sit in golden chairs. I can hardly make them out in the too bright light. Two holes gape open the palms of my hands. I am terrified. The queen with a kindly smile leans and puts a large pearl into the hole of my right palm, filling it. A glossy, polished anthracite has been put into my left palm. To my horror, it becomes a snake uncoiling.

Although the Apollonian head suggests sun and pulchritude, you can never get away with imagining psyche holds only what is beautiful and good. The snake is symbolic of chthonic wisdom because it is without feeling and profoundly instinctual—here, brought to life by spiritual fire, the uncoiling snake stirs within you.

Silver Lions

I am browsing through a pile of rugs for my house. Two are alike, but one is very different—a warm alizarin crimson I prefer. Suddenly, I'm outside—a plane on fire crashes in front of me. Then another and another. Destruction erupts everywhere. I don't know how to stop it or where anyone can flee for safety.

The carpet suggests being grounded by warm-toned feeling, which is your habitual way of being with others. But feeling can have a darker, problematic aspect. It can look at others with a jaundiced eye or turn against yourself a pejorative, rejecting judgment. The spiritual capacity to be above a situation in a way that enables an objective perspective, even from the ego, crashes.

My daughter-in-law asked me if I wanted to come along to put flowers on a grave. I picked up some roses, but they were stemless blooms and too fragile to carry, so I stayed home. When I left their house, looking back, I saw the entry lit up with a pair of silver couchant lions on each side of the front door.

"Whose grave is it?"

Something needed to die. The roses had been uprooted, no longer grounded in earthy reality. But there is movement ... the lions. Silver is lunar, feminine, but the lions are masculine and royal. Think about what this pair might mean for you.

When I was a teenager, I took the commuter train on Saturdays to study at the Chicago Art Institute. At the entrance steps still recline a magnificent pair of bronze lions. For me, they signify art and power.

Special Wine

Everyone has to leave, quickly, perhaps never to return. I can take only a few things. At the entry by the front door where I have piled my belongings, I notice a middle-aged man sitting at a small table in the hallway, drinking. Sadly, he pours the last of the bottle into his glass. I feel sorry for him. I have the selfsame special wine and pour him a glass. He looks at me with gratitude, nice-looking, well-enough dressed, rather dignified.

Telling her the dream, when I come to the moment of pouring him wine, my sight blurs.

The dream reflects a major change in you and in your relationship with the interior masculine. He, too, has changed. Instead of the derelict stealing matches from a bar, or the suspicious figure issuing from the back door of a church after dark, or the vagabond lying drunk on a pile of clothes in your basement, or one gleaming at you in his disheveled clothes—now he has dignity.

Turtle

Ripples in a pond. A resting, long-necked turtle no bigger than my hand, her carapace an artful pattern of many colors—I watch her. Suddenly, to my dismay, a strange, amorphous creature swallows her. A voice says, *Remember this!*

The turtle is amphibian, as is your writing, and its artistic shell shelters you. Given your perpetual haste, the turtle also intimates slow down, be observant. How dangerous your way of being is!—for your body, for your creativity, your soul, your attunement with the numinous psyche itself.

My time pressures? Yesterday. Managing the Jungian Magdalene event, mingling, relating to everyone, leaving at eight-thirty in the morning and getting home nine hours later, exhausted?

You have been swallowed by the amount of unconsciousness in many interactions.

She watched me with an ambiguous expression. Just before I left, she said sometimes she felt an impulse to sit beside me, to hold me. I left moved but puzzled. Why would she feel that way?

Three

Late! I hurry to get the elevator, step inside. It zooms to the top so fast I'm afraid I'll be killed. Then it drops, stops at the third floor—my destination.

This week I left my credit card at a restaurant and at another I lost my mother's three-pearl earring. Someone had stepped on the earring, dislodging one of the pearls, but the hostess found both. My life *was* a mad elevator ride!

Third floor, three pearls. Here, three signifies the feminine and your effort to embody it.

So many threes in my life! My father died when I was thirty, my life began to turn at 36, Jerry died when I was 69. At three, I jumped three times off the dock into the lake; the third time I was warned I was wearing my last dry clothes.

Well, you got their attention.

A man looks at me, laughs, snaps his fingers and turns a silver goblet into fire.

The Vase and the Rose

I hold a fluted, translucent vase of ancient Roman glass three feet tall.

A beautiful young woman appears in the center of a fire-lit fountain. Facing her, I am clutching a crimson rose. *Press it to your heart*, a man commands. I object. *It isn't white, purity's white. No,* he answers *It isn't.* When I press it against my heart, it punctures my hands and chest with thorns. It is painful.

You have begun to let others turn away from you, which is a sacrifice of the longing for acceptance and love. Conscious self-love can be painful.

She looked empathetic, concerned.

Poison Drifting Down, Flooding

I am outside at the back of a building when the enemy shoots causing poison to drift down. It covers my arms, my face. I shoot back, then flee into a shelter where a few people are packing to leave. Most of the furnishings being loaded onto a truck are mine. The war will continue. I wish I had brought some food.

How do we separate inner process from the world—politics, conflicts, the poison we breathe, the poison we listen to and watch, these cancerous assaults on our immune systems?

The war in this dream is personal. You still are being affected by the poison spread by the implacably ambitious poet of whom you were fond and whom you professionally supported. When attacked by her, you were so shocked and hurt, you failed to defend who you were and speak out about you all you had accomplished in the poetry world of which she and others were ignorant. Those poisonous fumes harmed you in the depths of self and soul, and in the poetry world.

My friend and I are sitting in the third row for a concert. Then in the lobby, she arranges to meet two people where she can show them her art. On the top floor (five stories up), I look below and see everyone in the lobby standing in water. The building is flooding, the stairs to the outside impassible. I wonder if we can get to the roof to be rescued.

In the dream you are above and able to gain a more objective perspective. Being removed, you are able to watch the woman below promoting her art, oblivious of the danger of collective unconsciousness. This is the work: in dreams, in reflection, in here.

Plumbing

At an ambitious friend's house, a workman discovers the blocked plumbing is related to a large hole in the bathroom that leads to a neighbor's bathroom on the opposite side of the street which he will also have to repair. I realize I have the same problem she has.

As before, you project onto a friend your shadow. Here, the shadow is a woman's ambition that has a blockage because it is tainted with unconscious motivations. It is a misuse of your deepest self to use your creative gift for ego prestige or importance. The plumber who can repair elemental workings is a laborer who has knowledge of how things work. He goes to the depths, beneath persona.

In a complex of beauty parlors, I enter an unfamiliar one by mistake. The hairdresser assumes I am coming to her. Feeling awkward and not wanting to hurt her feelings, I let her cut my hair, but the haircut and style are hideously wrong for me, and I am dismayed.

As you have described this friend, she would be comfortable with being beautiful and she would never allow someone to cut her hair unless it was a person she herself chose. She would say no to that hairdresser.

Above / Below

A woman beside me on the stairs gazes down at a poet standing surrounded by admirers. A voice says, *She controls everything; you can't engage with her.*

By gaining perspective, you distance yourself from your shadow. It splits, a positive woman beside you and the harmful one below. This is encouraging.

I climb a steep road with others passing me until I reach a rounded area at the top. A man warns me to be careful here because the ground can easily give way. I intuit that I was called here to dig. The earth cracks open. I look down into a pitch-dark cavity. Then inside it, I see a poet who has been through a life-threatening ordeal. She is wearing a blue blouse and skirt patterned with flowers and birds.

Recently, this dangerously ill woman told me that poetry, composing it, having it published and received, gave her strength and something to look forward to. She knows that she might die soon. In the depths of the Underworld exist both the pitch blackness of death and the source of living nature—the blue of spirit not above, but below.

The Musician

Even though we are still attracted to each other, a prestigious extroverted poet—once my muse—and I are going to separate.

The program is about a writer and a musician. The musician playing the piano never touches the keys. As he plays, he smiles at me.

For years he has come, a man I could not identify in a crowd yet whose reality I could feel without question—a presence, in this world but not of it.

A rather homely, tan-skinned woman stands on an empty stage. When the musician arrives, she sings with tears in her eyes. Her voice is very moving. At the end she tells the audience the lyrics came from the Bible, but she has forgotten what passage.

The singer is humble, expressing her feeling without performance. Her song is spiritual.

The Sacred Way

A young man who had been sleeping on a king-sized bed is taking a test. I interfere, telling the male observers to give him a good grade. Outside with my married poet friends, I watch a conflagration inside the house consuming everything, even the furniture. A silvery snake emerges from my bedsheets, disappears then reemerges elsewhere—electric, incandescent.

In this dream the heroic masculine youth will meet his challenge; you must trust him, trust his destiny. The fire in the interior of the house, combined with the silver electric snake in your bed, symbolize death. You must face this death consciously.

I am handed an age-darkened gold and phthalo green canoe with an ebony snake carved along the side. The snake's reared head shapes the prow.

I dreamed I composed a long narrative and titled it "Hello, Sacred Way." In the morning, I'd forgotten the narrative but realized it was a string of ordinary events.

ORGAN SYMPHONY

To see the acorn requires an eye for the image, an eye for the show, and the language to say what we see. ... When we are not looking with the eye of the heart ... we are failing to see the other person as bearer of an acorn of imaginative truth.

James Hillman

In the final analysis, we count for something only because of the essential we embody, and if we do not embody that, life is wasted.

C. G. Jung

The Charm

In a large indoor mall, I ask a woman the way out. She answers it depends on where you came in. I am not sure where I came in, but I have parked my car in a lot and have my keys. I walk in the direction to which she points when I discover in my pocket a child's gold chain with a charm and a tiny chest key. I want to return them but don't know to whom they belong.

This child's chain reminds me of the spinster's gift, the gilded chest with a pulsing heart inside. Is that the way out of the mall, the complex?

A young woman paints a very large canvas, but a man doesn't like it, so she paints another, an identical one on the same wall. I am cleaning something where a man is standing. Looking down, I notice that my white robe is smeared with black grease or charcoal. I don't know if it will wash out.

Part of this dream is about creativity, about the desire for artistic affirmation, but it's more complicated than that.

That evening I felt closer to myself than I have for a long time. It was as if the girl I was and the woman I am now are one being, as if part of my self has been asleep but preserved and unharmed, with nothing of her gusto and self-assurance lost.

If You Do Not Heed the Dream

With a companion, I am climbing a steep hill. We stop briefly. A bird flies at my face. Frightened, I turn away. He holds the bird cupped in his hands. I and the bird engage eye-to-eye. Then it flies away. We climb further when a sudden downpour forces us to flatten our backs against the slick face of a boulder.

The bird is alert to its territory, to borders, to danger. If you do not heed dreams, you will get caught in the downpour of the unconscious.

I hear scraping in the night, get up, and peer into the living room. A woman stands before a large canvas painting with a razor blade. Holding it, she turns toward me with a dark, fiery look. I am frightened. The canvas is black as pitch, painted in layers like lava, scraped and cut, dull and shiny. On it are three heads of wolves in a luminous, saturated yellow, the biggest right of center, the other two receding to the left. The smallest is a yellow-gold blur. The biggest is at half profile, its hair stiff, sharp, and pointy. Its amber eyes squint sidewise at me, a look fierce and terrifying.

Even now I can almost touch the glossy thickness of that paint, almost smell it. I see the intensity of the wolf's eyes, the fierceness of the woman's physical being.

The wolf is sacred, a spirit go-between the visible, collective world and the unknown depths.

ALPHA

A, a friend and composer, gives me a black box saying he has two of them, his and mine. Inside is an expensive camera with an elegant, unique lens. I am not sure how to use it.

This man is helping you live the rest of your life with the black container, an awareness of death. The camera is a vehicle for perception and a way for the ego to step aside, enabling objective observation. The alpha composer is introverted, serious, and spiritual, a replacement for the extroverted, worldly poet who used to be your muse. This is different from the notion that you have to deal with being judged at the end of your life as in the Egyptian Anubis myth.

Before the seven o'clock meeting, I swim in a university pool, its water warm and deep, mossy green.

Introversion does not mean to turn away from life. You are bathing in the warm pool of the universe, which is fertile green.

My extroverted friend says I should see a doctor for the growth on my face. She carries in her arms a newborn, who I am unable to care for because I can't find my stockings.

Your friend is telling you to see your doctor to work on your persona, your public image, because distraction and anxiety in extroverted situations lead you to get off-center. The newborn is an Adonis—a creative, vegetative god suggesting rebirth.

Victor

When I go to my parked car, a man sitting in the driver's seat claims it is his. Despite the new upholstery in the right-hand seat and only 15,000 miles on the gauge, I know it is mine. I write down the license plate: VICTOR. When he drives away, I push the panic button on my cell phone. A man with an Indian accent responds, and I cannot understand him. Victor reappears, stands cocky, condescending, laughing at my distress.

Transforming the negative animus is not an easy undertaking.

Transforming Fire

An older, lean Indian man with short, gray hair and I are intensely in love, but my husband pulls us apart and takes me to a high remote place for transportation out of the country. I stand there, alone. Suddenly, the Indian man hovers in the air, bringing me food. Again, we are together, and again my husband separates us. His gang binds me and takes away the man I love. Both of us feel great suffering.

This husband recalls my first husband, who was habitually critical of me, which over time undermined my youthful sense of self. Ultimately, it led to divorce.

Whatever undermines the ego of another person is abusive. The man in the dream who gangs up against you is hindering you from a connection with your inner spiritual masculine.

As if to prove the negative animus's power, for days I was depressed, reexperiencing old angers, feeling inferior to others, and seeing my creative life as worthless.

On horseback following a male rider, I suddenly realize that he has gone on while I have come to a spit of land at the edge of a wide, fast-flowing river. Looking to my left, I see he is being chased by a pack of wolves. The ground under my horse's hooves softens into a marsh. On the opposite bank I see more wolves. There seems to be no escape.

The meanings of wolves can be ambiguous and inclusive, carrying opposite implications but wolf packs are aggressive and deadly. The dark forces within the psyche are not personal. They will always exist as part of what Jung called the dark side of God.

A molten black mass bursts into flame. My hands catch fire. I feel them burning. My body scorches and solidifies like an anthracite corpse with white outlines. I am a ghost of myself. Hot, thirsty, disconsolate, I lie down in the dark where cool air issues from a cave. I feel the fur of a wolf brushing against my side as she moves slowly back and forth. I fall asleep. When I wake, I find a bowl of milk from which I drink. I fall back asleep. This happens three times, then I stand up. The darkness is no longer impenetrable.

Cooking Together

Today your anger is the worst I have ever seen in you. I feel tears inside.

What she saw was what she heard—old angers, ruminations over betrayals and losses. These flashes of past painful experiences and fury over what was done to me or what I failed to do to counter them or protect myself intrude uncannily, without outward provocation.

A man and I are cooking together.

It seems we are mixing, stirring, and boiling in the alembic of analysis over the heat of my rage. Perhaps the cooking will dissolve the anger and liberate me from the past.

With the owner, I am going through a house I intend to occupy. In the kitchen-dining area I notice deep marks on the floor by the sliding glass doors to the garden, marks that might be irreparable. Walking toward an exquisitely carved sideboard, she points to an expensive Persian rug. To my surprise and relief, she hands me a list of everything that is wrong for which I will not be held responsible.

From the beginning when you were hurt, you blamed yourself, and your anger sunk into that fiery dark where wolves attack you. You are not to blame for damage you did not cause.

Twelve

Two women and a man are in my house. The man is helping me make repairs. I rub oil into a wood table and show him some small holes in it. He tells me to do it later; he is about to leave. He embraces me, and we stay held in a magnetic intensity, breathing deeply as if we were one person.

This is a significant reversal. Two women in the house. You have rubbed oil into the table, making it beautiful despite the holes, and you are embraced.

I have made two mobile phone calls and I am about to make a third when a message comes up on my screen: You have twelve days.

Maybe that has been the urgency—I was going to die in twelve days, twelve months? I felt at ease with dying. So much of the past no longer mattered.

It may mean something else. The clock, wholeness, completion.

Mud Flood

Through the window I see a massive, rust-colored liquid mud stretching to a flat horizon and flowing toward us. Hurriedly, I change and dress the baby. The man decides we must flee. I grab her, clothes, and bottles of milk. No time to heat one.

Here is a birth of new life, wholeness in its infancy. Alert to danger, you act instinctively to protect it.

I am living in an old wood house of many rooms with trees and abundant vegetation. After being gone a few days, I discover the baby swaddled on a pallet by the front door. She hasn't been fed, and I am dismayed. I carry her into the house to feed her.

You have come home to care for your own child. She is both the child you were and remain within, and a transformation that in psyche symbolizes the enfolding of the ego within the Self.

Orange Zinnias

Walking between rows of old-fashioned school desk-seats where students are writing, I abruptly chop in half with a hatchet a bright orange snake lying on a desktop.

Those desks! Fourth grade? The family's traumatic move to a new town and a school where I didn't fit.

The snake was poisonous despite its bright orange appearance.

At the house of an ambitious poet—slight friend, slight disparager, I can't go to the toilet because it is stopped up and flooded. The laundry I washed did not wring out, so I have to wring it by hand, piece by piece. At the end of my bed, yellow and orange zinnias have been arranged in a frame.

Why do I have to keep doing this, going through the same shadowy issues?

The automatic machine isn't adequate. You still have to wring the laundry out by hand, consciously, piece by piece. When you do, the snake is transformed. The orange zinnias can be arranged aesthetically in a frame. They suggest warmth, feeling, intuition, and the feminine aspects of the sun.

Pink Tree

With two women at the top of a snow-covered pro-
minence, I begin to descend, but it becomes scarily rapid,
as if I am on a snowboard. I come to a halt before the
last, gradual slope where I offer to carry one woman's
dress heels. At first she demurs but then lets me carry
them. They have a strong smell of feet. She is sparkling,
happy because of something she has accomplished. The
land here belongs to the other woman.

Maybe these are good companions, women who are grounded,
happy and able to be creative.

*No, you give too much, carry someone else's dress shoes, which stink.
Your complex gets triggered, your fear of broken relationship, of
betrayal, of being again deserted and left alone.*

I, or the woman with me, invite two men to dine with
us. Afterward, one of the men complains about the food.
Everyone expects me to pay for the meal, which I had
not intended.

*As a feeling introvert, you can be manipulated by others' logic.
Because your temperament is fluid, warm, and generous, you need
the observant animus. With his discernment, you can give yourself
time and space to feel and think through what others demand.
Without that, you give too much, which results in being resentful or
angry.*

In the center of a canvas I paint a bright pink tree trunk
with a blossom of cheerful, variegated green leaves.

Yellow Tents

After a gathering at my friends' spacious second home, I pick up whatever has been left lying about and prepare to depart but I can't locate my belongings. A man helps me find them. He and I and another woman hang on to the siderails in a boat that plunges steeply downward. Below and ahead the river rushes into a large body of water. I realize that even if we make it alive, I will never be able to return.

In gatherings you have played the role of the servant, which makes it difficult to find what truly belongs to you. You have made dramatic changes. You won't go back to what you have been, but the descent is risky, the process incomplete.

At the end of an outdoor concert, my daughter and I applaud, but no one else does because the program is religious. We become separated in the departing crowd. I think I know the way, then slip into a sandpit grasping at rocks that dislodge and fall. A bearded, semibald guy uses his funky old truck and a rope to pull me out. I go toward the parking lot, where the crowds are thinning. I don't have my cell phone or my purse. To my left I pass closed shop stalls covered by yellow tents in the rain. I despair.

Panic

Ticket in hand, I am waiting in a complex for a flight leaving in two hours. I want to ship twin beds. I search for an agent to handle the order, but people are occupied, and airport employees do not know where to send me. Outside, no one can help me. Twice I try the same route, but it leads nowhere. I take a different road and find myself by black water lapping medieval walls. A boy wades out of the water toward me. I return to where I started when I see a rainbow-colored searchlight arcing back and forth. I decide this is the direction I should go. I will cancel the shipping order. A sandy-haired man wearing a brown jacket and carrying a brown leather briefcase offers to go with me.

I woke terrified, taking quick, gasping breaths.

You are leaving the way you have been. The beds are just furniture, a metaphor for trivia or preoccupation with worldly affairs. What the dream does is touch a complex, and you are leaving for a more personal, individual, deeper, inward way to be. No one can guide you; you go around in circles and can't find your way. The boy emerging from black water in a medieval setting suggests the black death, the plague. Here is your terror, your fear of helplessness. The ego feels in jeopardy because it cannot control when death comes. But two elements in the dream are powerful: the searchlight of many colors and the man wearing warm, earthy tones carrying something important that will be with you in this transition.

Tantric Red

In grandmother's home I meet a dark-haired, well-built, virile, creative, literary man. We get into bed naked, kissing passionately, when two women enter the room. The blond younger woman is looking for my friend to do something for her mother. *All of you get out of my grandmother's bedroom!* I exclaim. My grandmother smiles in approval. The blond shows me broken pieces of rose-gold jewelry that belonged to her mother. She wants me to fix them, but the tiny pieces fall to the floor. I bend down to pick them up, wondering, *Why am I doing this?* I look up, seeing my lover, dressed, going out the door.

You cannot repair what was broken in your mother. The wise old woman approves of your telling everyone to get out. These immature, undeveloped women represent people and events that get in the way of having a realized emotional connection with the masculine in yourself.

I am writing a prose journal of my analysis. A man points out I am repeating myself; the writing's not imaginative. Then I draw picture words that look like ink with water on paper, the images amorphous, intriguing.

How can I be poetic when what prose requires most is clarity and precision for communication, not a Rorschach with infinite possible interpretations? Is this critical man helpful? Maybe I need to sort out when a dream should be rejected. Maybe dreams issue from dark as well as light forces? Or maybe it is time to return to poetry?

A creative woman, a novelist who lives simply, intro-
duces me to a male writer. I don't care about being old.
He excites me. We embrace and want to have sex.
Strangers enter her studio. He and I go into the bath-
room and lie down on a two-toned vermillion and
magenta rug. Kiss.

The Woman from the Sea

A tall, graceful woman steps onto the beach from the sea carrying a pottery bowl with a green plant. She talks of Goodman, a film director who has helped a dramatic company. She takes me to meet them gathered in a private house. The street that leads to it goes between high resort hotel walls. I tell her I know unknown places by the sea that I can show her.

You and she share a connection with the watery depths from which life is born. Green is living, being alive, but also death. You have been afraid of imminent death, but this is theater. It suggests death and rebirth. Venus emerging from the sea.

Listening to music, I watch others dance, then dance myself with three men who seem fond of me. A willowy woman wearing a lovely soft green dress sees a spot on it. With a penlike object she touches the spot, and it disappears.

You are more at ease with yourself, more soulful. You aren't talking about a goal or what you have to do. You are free to enjoy your children, your chosen commitments, your writing friends. You do not have to justify your life.

I realized the pen acts like magic.

The Tree of Life

With a man in his early forties, I enter an assembly where
people have gathered to argue a case. In opposite semi-
circles men stand to the left, women to the right,
between them a long wood table. The man with whom
I entered joins the men at the far end. To my surprise I
learn that he is the chief lawyer. There is a great, ancient
tree that they want to get rid of. Cutting it down is a
dilemma. If it falls to the left, it will destroy the house;
if it falls to the right, three rectangular formations to
hold water will be clogged, making the communal
reservoir unusable. I have warm feelings about the tree
and do not want it cut down. The headman tells me I
am not allowed to speak, and the woman opposite him
wants someone to shoot my legs so I cannot move.

Is the tree in some way a threat to the community, the collective?
The dream is a mystery to me yet feels crucial, as if something
much greater than my personal life is at stake.

*You are an actor in this performance and must speak to defend the
tree, despite the headman, who is cut off from instinct and feeling,
and the woman who must conform. The tree's girth is too large, its
roots too widely spread, its branches too glorious to be sacrificed.*

The Question

I am going to sell my house, but I am frustrated because I can't get through to the agent on the phone. I have been living with a family, and the father has offered to give me a ride to the city. The mother has no reaction to my leaving. In order to get her to respond, I announce, *I am leaving for good!* I gather my things and try to kiss her cheek as I leave, but she is remote, unapproachable. I feel a bewildering ache.

I wonder if this indifferent mother is my analyst.

The analyst brings two other patients into the room. I look at the clock. I came at 4:10. It is 4:40, and I am supposed to leave at five. *Do you want me to leave? No,* she says. I object to having others in the room.

The other patients are your own distractions. I listen to whatever you bring in.

An analyst asks me to paint a picture, but when I do she comments that she doesn't like the dark blues and purples. She makes a paper chain of bright colors to fix onto my picture, which upsets me because the darker colors fit my mood.

Your expression shows discontent. Do you feel I am not empathetic?

My mother and sister have already gone. A grossly overweight woman in black comes and sits herself down, not to be ignored. A man and I are about to leave.

That fat female is always hungry, devouring, impossible to ignore. My mother and sister are dead. Perhaps she is death.

The obese woman in black does suggest death but when you are split off from the ability to know what you need—the basic early needs—safety, nourishment, love—it leads to agitation. The mother and sister go away, which leaves the fat woman isolated. Imagine how she feels. What will heal her?

In the office of a woman analyst, I hold a scallop shell with pearly nacre that I have been given. She leans forward saying, *Don't you understand what this means?* She selects two books for me to read and then, after a thought, adds a third, a colorful, image-filled journal. Outside, I go down the street, but it feels wrong. Someone says the church I am looking for is the opposite way, to the left.

The gesture of your hand holding the shell was open, freely giving. The shell is both feminine and of the sea, evoking the birth of the goddess of love. The church, your soul's home, is to the left; that is, inward.

Cancer

One of four who live in the house has breast cancer.

My mother drowns herself in alcohol.

At the theater my mother is so drunk we have to carry her out. A man is watching.

My mother never drank. Alcohol poisoned her Welsh father's life. She inherited spiritual strength from her grandmother, who was a Seneca Falls Prohibitionist, a widow and an ordained minister.

You have been too much the Mother. The effect on you is poisonous.

While I'm taking a test, the professor, viewing me as a superior student, takes me aside to do work for him, so I begin the test late. Others are already swimming. I swim out to where they are, but the water becomes so heavy I can barely keep my head above it. I call for help. He and others rescue me.

Being separated out as superior leads to trouble for you. On the other hand, the teacher recognized your unique value. When you try to be as others are, you nearly drown.

Empyrean

Returning after weeks away, I put my clothes in drawers and push a small backpack into the top shelf of the closet. My bed is unmade. I speculate that the man I like has left it this way intentionally. When he comes, putting his arm around my shoulders, we go for a walk. He points to the night sky. Behind the bare limbs of a great tree I see a fiery galaxy—enormous, amoeboid, glowing yellow-gold along the edges. Gradually, it loses intensity, fades.

When you first came to me, you were anxious and driven, closing in. Today you are radiant.

The Silk Gown

Loafing on the floor facing a cat who says, *I love you*. He can talk! I am amazed.

My black Persian was a gift from my daughter, who wanted me to be with some living creature now that I am old and living alone.

The miracle is softness, being in tune with yourself.

I am dressed in a silk gown with gold embroidery and a red half-moon design, a royal red strip down the front—a gift.

One Drama in Three Acts

My grandson is sitting with me outside listening to Eric Satie. I am holding my cat, who gets agitated, wants to escape. I am trying to figure out a problem: Three roads circle three structures, but something is missing. After the music is over, we cross the street and climb steps a hill when I notice my cat is gone. I call and call, then go back down the steps in the dark to find him. Crossing the street, I sense then see large, black and white feral dogs roaming.

~

Flying alone down the coast, low over verdant valleys and hillocks that become higher, more forbidding, short of my destination, I must land. As I descend, I fly over three men who look up and I imagine they will be impressed to see a white-haired woman pilot. I land and, walking away from the plane, I begin to climb passing walls of steep sandstone. I come to a couple in an encampment surrounded by iron ore rock formations. He is grilling some kind of meat and offers me a piece almost raw, which I accept but do not eat. She gives me three of her six handmade art/poetry books, each unique and quite good. I demur at her giving me so many. When I leave, unsure of my way, a great swarm of black birds fly from a cavernous cave mouth. I am afraid I won't find my way home.

~

Hurrying across sand that gives way under my feet, I reach a mountainside trail that rises above the sea. A great hawk flies overhead, then perches, watching me. Hungry, I come to a small clearing. On a stone slab I find a bowl of water and some nuts. I climb to a high place

140

by a stream, where I drink and fall asleep. When I wake, the stars are brilliant, and an owl stares at me. At dawn I continue until the trail comes to a dead end in blackberry bushes. I despair. Below, a woman in feather white with a child, looks up, pointing to me. I start down toward them but when I reach the path, they are gone. The way is wider, more traveled. Midmorning the light becomes too bright to see. I stand, paralyzed. A male voice says, *Walk into it*. I take a few steps, stop, step again, stop. Afraid, surrounded by throbbing intense light. I remember Jerry as he was dying, telling me, *Go through the light*. Again, I walk step by step, looking down, watching my feet. Gradually, the light begins to thin. A woman's arms wrap me in a soft-spun shawl. A masculine voice says, *You will never be alone*.

Two-Sided Mirror

He shows me a full-length mirror on a lead stand that flips over. With it I can see both my front and my back side.

He carries a child, hands her to me saying, *She's yours and she's been hurt.*

He knows I have discovered the secret, wants me to bury it. I wrap it, hide it to keep it safe. It will stay with me through the crossing over into death. It seemed I hid a pulsing heart.

Power Washed

The man next door asks me to move my car because workmen are going to power-wash his house. When I go to move my car, I can't because the whole neighborhood is covered in snow.

You can't go anywhere and you don't have to do anything. It is being done for you. You can rest the way people who are snowed in have to stop going to work. In alchemy whitening is a sign of increased consciousness.

High Fidelity

Pilots coming in to land, their wings nearly touching the treetops. A brilliant diamond light emanates from the interior of their white airplanes. As they land, they fold their wings like insects.

The inner diamond light, the wings like insects' wings, the white planes reflect instinctual masculine spirituality.

Dressed in white with silver armor, my head uncovered, I am a beaming youth with bountiful light brown hair— not me and yet me.

The struggle not to succumb to automatic reactions to others has changed you. You are lighter, more youthful.

It's a ziggurat! I exclaim, looking up at a wood housing structure with people climbing and descending outside stairs. I have to leap and hang on to a rod to get the first level. Half way up I meet Robert Duncan. We discuss a performance we are supposed give with woman who hasn't arrived.

I once interviewed Robert Duncan in his high, narrow Victorian in San Francisco. He had a metaphysical bent and, I believe, would have considered the word *ziggurat* spiritual. At times a ziggurat had a shrine or temple at the top.

Upstairs in my house, a man in the loft is fixing the connection so my hi-fi will work.

The Ambiguity of Dreams

Standing at the back of a balcony watching a performance below on the circular floor, I see a gunman enter from the shadows. Suddenly, he begins shooting, killing many but not the dancers' instructor, a poet. She stands in the center wearing a floor-length white sheath with pastel flowers. I tell her I can offer her wisdom, but she looks at me disdainfully, saying, *I don't need your wisdom.*

The instructor in the dream resembles the woman from my past who has haunted my psyche for decades, once a close friend whose drastic misperceptions and devastating actions caused me physical and mental agony. Here, she is transformed, lovely.

Even so, she is disdainful. Idealized, perhaps? If so, she remains a danger to the soul.

Isadora's Scarf

Leaving a resort hotel, I am aware of wearing a dramatic, sheer, body-fitting outfit and trailing a long, Duncanlike, sparkly silk scarf, but I don't have my expensive jacket. I think it might be one I saw folded on an upper shelf in the hotel room, the shelf I couldn't reach.

Isadora Duncan, her freedom with her body—how desirable! On the other hand, her scarf strangled her.

I am with a woman therapist, but it feels no longer necessary. She suggests I join her group sessions. I don't want that.

Outside, I find a loose board on the back of my house, under a small window. I dig it free with my fingers. A man sees behind the board wood that it is rotten. He will repair it.

Apparently, there remained minor work to be done on the wall between the interior and the outer world, and the window itself. I decided I can do this alone, without her.

It isn't finished. The border, the house with the wood rot on the outside needs repair.

Milk Glass Compote

A woman attacks me then pursues me into the garage, howling. I call out feebly, *Help, help*. I fumble with my phone. Face to face, her expression distorted, catlike, she scratches me, her hands claws.

The day before this dream a woman was aggressively hostile. With conscious determination, I contained my own reaction. I listened and kept guard not to counterattack. I felt my whole response, felt the fury trembling inside. This was dramatically different from the repression of my childhood. Mulling it over, I thought I should have defended myself.

You were strong enough to withstand attack and let the other speak, albeit in an unrestrained and unreflective way. We need to work on getting you strong enough to say, "You can't talk to me that way," strong enough risk rejection and loss.

~

I'm late and, without checking my hair or makeup, I rush to leave, locking the door, then realize I left my purse inside. I go anyway to the dance where the man I love is waiting.

I offer a milk glass compote with fruit to the icon of a goddess. A woman standing behind me holds me in embracing arms.

My daughter wrote instructions: *My mother must breathe and be able to drink water, or she will die.*

Some people bless our lives.

Ship Rock

When others contradict who I am, the picture gets blurred. I get confused, my mind is a maelstrom.

When conflict occurs, the jumble in your thinking, the emotional overload, the feeling of helplessness go back to childhood trauma.

If you stay empathetic, you can be related even when someone is aggressive. At the same time, you must not merge with the other. Valid empathy requires separation, the ability to stay aware of your subjective self.

After an encounter with another angry person, I discovered that I could step back, could sense my core. I realized that when a volcano erupts near me and the ground shakes and I am no longer sure of what is true, I can give space for what I do not know, in myself as well as in the other person.

I take a photo of a rock island the shape of a ship facing a rough, heaving sea. Imagining that one day the sea will overwhelm it, I want to record what withstood life's storms.

Gold Medallions

I cast the I Ching coins: K'an: Difficulty at the Beginning. It warned no premature move. Do not remain alone. It is wise to delegate what must be done. All is struggling to attain form, to bring order out of confusion. The tender green shoot has sprouted at the edge of a large rock. Well-rooted, it will grow as long as it has water and sun.

Seven embossed gold medallions suspended in dark space. A man beside me is helping me find the one that is missing.

We are standing on natural shelves in the flank of a steep cliff. Anchored above, I cling to a rope with a child in my arms, trying to get to down. It is arduous.

My only sorcery is an emblem I can carry for the rest of my life, a symbol—a coin, a circle within a circle, inside an infinity of spiraling coils.

A man measures my waist, says it was 24 now it is 54.

The five and the four are symbolic of both grounding and transcendence. Care of the child is crucial. This is the promise, the potential.

Heading East

Driving with Karol, I stop on our way to go to a conference, where we take two seats among the twenty-five set up. Hungry, she leaves to find something to eat. Others arrive and take her seat. They talk among themselves, but all fall silent when the speaker narrates the story of her love affair, including how her lover drove in a speed boat, dragging her three children clinging to ropes. She could see they were drowning, the boy emerging from the water with his eyes closed then sinking again. I leave to find Karol and to get directions. I know we are heading east. No one knows the way. I try to get a map on Karol's cell phone but realize I have only its shell. I look everywhere, but her phone is gone along with all her personal information.

My college roommate and one of my dearest friends, Karol, who was an agnostic stoic, has been dead for over ten years. Her alcoholic, gambler first husband deserted her and their children, leaving them destitute. Although once she tried suicide, with great courage, she survived.

In death, nothing personal remains. For you, this is the journey east, toward the rising sun of a different day.

Tsunami

Caught in high waves, I am struggling to keep alive a baby who has been submerged and to swim to shore.

A man and I dive down, touching the seafloor, and rise again to the surface.

From a third- or fourth-floor window I see that the waves are rising so high they endanger cars and people below. A huge wall of incoming wave bucks and heaves toward shore. We race to leave the building. I do not know if we have time enough to escape.

The threat of the tsunami reflects a response to the world's catastrophic mayhem, and it is simultaneously a warning of potential interior danger.

Urgency

Having entered a university church, a faded red fresco inside, medieval-feeling, cold and empty, I leave by a different door. Walking downhill, I find myself on an unfamiliar street, and no matter where I search I cannot find my car.

It's frustrating! After all these years of psychological work, the dreams make me feel as if I still can't find my center, my spiritual home.

We have known for a long time that traditional Christianity no longer can be a living experience for you. Your work now, after the personal work is mostly done, is to find what's missing. This is especially urgent late in life.

I have come to give a reading of my manuscript, *The Transformation*, but I can't find it. *I can't lose it! It's five years of work!* No one responds. After the room empties, I find it and ask the reading series director if I can come back to read it. *Not for nine months*, he replies.

– a pregnancy.

The Dark Powers

I am walking outdoors with a man who suggests we hike up a reddish gully to a path that leads to the main road along the hill's crest, our destination. That's an interesting idea. I've never gone that way. I notice clouds darkening to my left. Halfway, a flashflood gushes into the gully. Almost drowning, he climbs onto my back. I swim toward the embankment where we had entered. I reach it with a last, fugitive, heave.

This animus has been on your back for years.

I'm inside a large space with rough wood walls and barnlike doors on all four sides. One at the back, opposite the main entry, opens. A creature rushes in, his torso human, but below the waist he is a hoofed animal. He has been changed into this deformity by malevolent beings. He looks deranged, wild, agonized but not dangerous. Others start to follow him into the room. Something blocks their way. It will force this creature back as well. I sense similar horrors exist behind the other doors. I am in danger. If they capture me, I too will be transformed in this cruel way.

The animal-men are fragile, weak, unable to walk upright. The dark forces in the unconscious cannot be controlled. They exist in the psyche and in the world as well. By being aware of this reality, you can live freely and not become a victim of them. In the earlier dream, you ignored the storm clouds and followed, unreflectingly, the dominating masculine within you. The red gully was a wound in the earth, and the earth embodies the feminine. Wounded, that feminine is vulnerable to torrential flood.

Through the Window

Inside a screened-in porch with my cat, I watch a gray wolf poke her nose through the screen. Terrified, I stab a stick into her throat. Seeing sadness in her eyes, I realize she was never a threat. I take her to the vet, who says he can cure the wound, but the wolf will have to stay with him for several days.

I am appalled at what ignorance and fear led me to do, even in a dream. How long it takes to integrate a spirit animal into one's being!

In the upstairs living room, my grandson helps me move an alizarin crimson carpet away from the center. I see it is mostly worn through. My friend comes in from work wearing a rich blue-green fitted dress, her hair short and youthful-looking. She moves a table near the window for better light.

That crimson carpet suggests feeling no longer dominates your life.

Four Kings

A handsome, sandy-haired, British-looking gentleman and I are attracted to each other. He moves close to me although he'd arrived with others, including a woman with short black hair who glares at us. Again, I am with this man, this time alone. We embrace, and he ejects some semen.

The Brits are accustomed to handling authority in a composed, self-assured way. He makes a good animus companion.

I am with four larger-than-life kings dressed in ancient garb. I go to a program and sit one row above a relative and her nuclear family, aware of being left out. When I leave, a woman seeing me lights up happily, saying, *Hi.*

Your good connection with the feminine is expressed by the response of the friend. It compensates for what cannot happen with this self-contained, nuclear family. These kings appear as archetypal masculine authority. They belong to the Self and offer a sense of solidity and authority. Four is a symbol for wholeness.

Organ Symphony

A woman who resembles the poet-nemesis of my past stands in the center of a stage, transformed into a fair-haired beauty in a white fitted gown printed with pastel flowers. A man wants to assassinate her. From the balcony above, I shoot him.

This assassin derives his impulse from the Furies who come from the dark maternal instinct to demand revenge. This time you, as ego, stop him, meanwhile the poet herself has been transformed into a gentle feminine figure.

Simultaneously with my friend's work on a major composition, I decide to write a work to be choreo-graphed for Saint-Saëns' Organ Symphony. It will have that rich melodic texture and begin in silence: *Do you hear it? the whispering.* ... I open a door and enter the room where I will be working. A male analyst friend and two or three other analysts I know are in a meeting. I am going to leave, but they say they are almost finished and I do not have to leave.

I have found where I belong and regained what I experienced as a child. When I was very young, I spent hours behind the great pipes listening to them breathe as the church organist practiced and played whatever he desired. In Saint-Saëns' piece, when the organ breaks through the orchestra like a thunderous stroke, the vibrations stir in me, in many others, a deeply felt, mysteriously sacred thrill.

A Black Blacker Than Black

I dreamed a man who desired me tied me, then hung me dangling over the rock ledge, the rope connected to the knife he'd stabbed into my heart.

I dreamed a man, discouraged, painted over his art. I had come too late to help him.

I dreamed the watchmaker repaired my watch, replacing the defective part with a shining piece that would last forever.

The animus manifests in opposite ways, one dark and destructive, the other light-bringing. The Self is blackness as surely as it is brilliance. The watchmaker has the power to transform the blacker-than-black until black itself is luminous.

The Cat and the Lily

A kitten shows up inside my house. She needs to be fed. I go to the kitchen to see what I can find for a kitten. My cat begins to nurse her.

Like the infant in dreams, the cat is part of the immortal self.

When I come downstairs, I am astonished. The lily, which had been small and uneventful for a long time, had grown a tall strong stem and bloomed, its flower a rich crimson with an erect yellow stamen.

Long after the dream I sensed its presence—numinous, drenched in color, life-affirming.

The Gift

At home in the dark, longing for I knew not what, I dropped down into a meditative stillness, hoping my guide would come. I heard a woman's voice:

Do you see me? Before me she stands—tall and willowy in a lightly spun, full-length gown tinted a subtle shade of sunset green. She holds in her hands a large sphere made of shimmering, silvery gold-flecked particles that emanate light. *Put your hand into it.* I do, thinking, *This is impossible.* Finding no resistance, my hand, wrist, and forearm disappear, becoming part of it. I withdraw my hand, expecting all will be as it was. My hand, wrist, and forearm have been transmuted into that same strange substance. Then I watch, amazed as it begins to flow through me until my whole body is luminescent.

It flowed, transforming me into all that was me and all that was not me. Then in a voice not human, I heard the word *KINDNESS* and I understood what she had been trying to give me from the beginning.

AS I HAVE DONE

I dwell in the spirit's calm nothing can move
And watch the actions of Thy vast world-force,
Its mighty wings that through infinity move
And the Time-gallopings of the deathless Horse.

Sri Aurbindo

Now that I am done
  no child needs   no calling beckons
I am a wanderer in this house

This candle with its perfect calm
this Kuan Yin with a long sleeve
  draped over her bent wrist
this miniature tree with its permanent green

These were my response to her command
  she who never touches my hand
Make me a shrine
  voice none but I could hear

This *she*   once a person – consoler   guide –
  now herself and elsewhere
does she pause at the closed door
  think of me   then turn away
as I have done?

This is a grassland I am crossing
   a riverbed   not a road
where others come and go

my van is white
my belongings within

I pull aside pause
   to watch the wings
that through infinity move

then swiftly fall
   afraid
I'd opened that door
   too wide

The home I sought was never home
Such is the irony of perception

How long it took me to learn!
All I had to do was step out of the sleeping form

Reflecting above all that was and all that isn't
can make heart's turmoil—even that! a dwelling

Even wine can't heal this dizziness

I go out imagining only I can do what must be done
unasked   uncalled for

I am the water-fountain   its pump clogged by debris
Why do I believe I am a communal well?

I go out knowing the exhaustion to which I return
What magic could fit my brain to my brittle bones?

I'm tired   very tired   an old widow-bird
Any moment the voice will declare   *Done!*

Rushing back frantic you asked. . .
   a waiter's irritated *No*
Looking pleased the hostess turned away
   retrieved the glasses she'd set aside

Your ticket in hand . . . *oh matinée!*
Bemused the usher guided you to the opposite side
   a single vacant seat beside your friends

Late night dark heading toward BART
   through Tenderloin spillover a middle-aged couple
appeared accompanied you
   then disappeared

as if every moment is watched over

It's easy to fall off the ends of the earth
   when the intentional foot   crossed by a cat
stalls midair above the stair

It's likely when you die no one
   will remember Mom and Dad
No one will remember you
   Imagine that!

Imagine being a beam of light
   This morning's too bright to trust
When a door opens the alarm goes berserk

Halfway across the arched bridge
   you see no reflection in the turmoil
carried relentlessly toward that yearning ocean
   some call home

Brow furrowed with effort
   an infant stares into your gaze
where question is mirrored

One day you slept till noon
drugged by medications paired with wine

Wary   emerging
then aware yesterday's docility
   neither harmed   nor healed

Each breath began nothing
   each step went nowhere
To your needing friend your voice
   could not conceal its vexed edge

Sun warming your hand where the rings were
warns   for you it is evening

This is how I'm answered
four dreams in one night

In the first I slid a brass bolt against raucous street guys
Hearing my thoughts   one whirled toward my door

In the second I wandered inside Hammer Mountain
     Thor's cathedral of stone
then lost my way in urine stained snow

In the third I folded bright white linen
     for the ever-sleeping queen
then servant-like folded ruby velvet
     for the waiting king

In the last Mother in her jonquil-yellow dress
     drove the two of us southward
toward the gulf through green fields

How frustrating it must be for the Master
to have no other language

Too soon what's done
seems wrong

A fragment of day batters the brain
with its broken maul

then from nowhere
comes core-deep tolling

tolling at noon
calling us home

and hearing
we trust what has no sound

as if we had been gathered here
solely for this

Why no tears?
What beckons you?

What prompts you
  to catch each moment at the crest?
You ride it   this great final wave
  a surfer loving the thrill

On impulse you bought silk
  harem pants   chartreuse
Near dawn you rise drawn toward
  a mysterious blinking light

Her dream— searching for her horse
both fields empty

How bereft her look   bereft
    and burdened by question
How hold emptiness

How endure when mind disrupts
    instinctual rest
and remorse makes of night a wake

How wait . . . for a thought
    a twist of thought
too subtle to stir chimes into sound

Out of nothing   would it burst forth
    sinew flank muscle and mane
leap   flaring its wings in visible air

When the finch trapped inside knocked
   her beak against that frantic glass
I was the heart wildly beating

I know that knocking
I know how terrifying it is

Cupping her softness in my hands
   I elbowed aside the sliding door
She flung herself into brilliance

I know that knocking
I know the warmth that carried me
   here where I can breathe

About some compensating
  subtle change as the body wanes
the aging speaker and I agree

Asked he named it
  forgivingness
The word *surrender*
  came to me

surrender to the stumbles
  the avalanche of errors
the worn-thin entrance ticket lost
  as was his wife's mind

What had he surrendered to?
What infused his flushed
  embarrassed smile?

Did he know he was warming
listeners in that cold white room
  with his sweetness?

This is that time you are told to relax
    in the leisure of old age
that time when rainwater pouring
                        down the stairs
    floods inside your house
warning it's time to break through
    whatever has made you habitual

A gifted woman obediently sorts laundry
    stacked in immense piles on the basement floor
and the dream-I gathers up more to bring her

In a dream you're stashing your jewelry
    in a hard-to-reach drawer
then sit at a last home table with the decrepit
    for a breakfast of whatever is served

There is no escape from dreams
    no escape from a lifetime of cause
as when the after-effect of conflict
    with an intractable friend
bleeds into blame for having betrayed yourself
    not checking your calendar
the promise to be where you wanted to be
    and you fooled your time away

This is that time of aging when failure to attend
    can cost your life
that time when you fear a fear that will overwhelm you

This is that time barely-there fog dims finities
inside the ivy-walled border   absolute clarity

Lit fog on an upper gate-arc edge
  under falls of branchlets on the verge
you go through   go beyond
  into what air-density makes remote

Uncanny   that sense of it   the in-between of it
 was – is   long ago – now
born in your body

while inside the outside
migrants seed-picking between the cracks
  proclaim not dying   not not dying

This is that seldom found time   reposeful
    your feet resting on soft calf's leather
warming in mid-morning light

Fragile webs of cloud shape and reshape
    moving in slow motion southward
Billions of billions of sunlit particles   a field
    of delicate blue like a peaceful mind

What could there be to regret
    when words come in their natural order
when what has been planted in the psyche
    leads to fruition that does not decay

like chimes heard from a great distance
    then not heard
then heard in memory's placeless air

The warp   white wool carded into yarn
the weft   dyed ocean hues
     turquoise lavenders peacock blues

The width determined by a carpenter
the length just right to hang
     ceiling to craft shop floor

The pattern variations upon a theme
     by whim or like Atropos
she chose as she wove

As if young dreams fulfil themselves
     here
I rest my feet on the sea

CPSIA information can be obtained
at www.ICGtesting.com
Printed in the USA
BVHW071419010619
549897BV00003B/148/P